Morality is of course part of ethics, but it is not the whole of ethics. Morality is about some of our responsibilities to others, whereas ethics is about one's 'ethos', one's whole way of life. It is about what sort of person one is.
Anthony Grayling
The Heart of Things

An AVA book

published by

AVA Publishing SA
Rue des Fontenailles 16
Case Postale
1000 Lausanne 6
Switzerland

t: +41 786 005 109
e: enquiries@avabooks.ch

distributed by

ex-North America
Thames & Hudson
181a High Holborn
London WC1V 7QX
United Kingdom

t: +44 20 7845 5000
f: +44 20 7845 5055
e: sales@thameshudson.co.uk
www.thamesandhudson.com

USA and Canada
Watson-Guptill Publications
770 Broadway
New York
New York 10003
USA

f: +1 646 654 5487
e: info@watsonguptill.com
www.watsonguptill.com

English Language Support Office
AVA Publishing (UK) Ltd

t: +44 1903 204 455
e: enquiries@avabooks.co.uk

designed by

Lucienne Roberts
sans+baum

production and separations by

AVA Book Production Pte Ltd
Singapore

t: +65 6334 8173
f: +65 6259 9830
e: production@avabooks.com.sg

ISBN
2 940373 14 0 and
9 782940373 14 7

10 9 8 7 6 5 4 3 2 1

Good:
An introduction to ethics in graphic design
Lucienne Roberts +
Consider this simple conundrum:
is it possible to be a **bad good designer**
or a **good bad designer** for that matter?
If the answer is 'yes' then which is preferable
and what does this reveal about the
relationship of ethics to graphic design?
Graphic design is in **ethical flux**. There
is disenchantment with style-led solutions
and the pursuit of self-expression alone.
Manifestos and themed publications have
raised awareness of 'design for good',
but the debate about what the term means
is in its infancy.
This book sets out a basis for
designers, educators and students to consider
the **values** and the **potential** of the profession.
Designers are people. The decisions we
make define who we are. Our ethical choices
help shape the world.

Contents

Using this book

Ethics isn't a black-and-white subject.
Neither is this book – there are lots of greys.

This book opens with an introduction and
closes with reference material. There are five
sections in between. Sections 1, 2 and 3 are
theoretical. Sections 4 and 5 are practice-based.

Each section has an opening
page that looks like this.

Section 1: Making good
An illustrated history section.

Section 2: Approaching good
A theoretical section that
includes four interviews. Each
opens with a portrait of the
interviewee, followed by their
interview.

Section 2 also includes a
glossary and the human rights
outlined in the British Human
Rights Act.

Section 3: Debating good
A theoretical section made up
of five essays. Each opens
with an illustration followed
by the essay.

Section 4: Being good
A practice-based section including five interviews with practitioners who work in design and related fields.

Section 4 also includes answers by ten graphic designers to the question 'Are you a good designer?'.

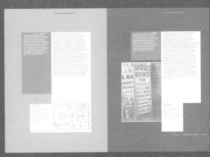

Section 5: Doing good
A practice-based section that uses a new mapping system to explore sustainability in design work.

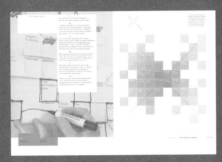

Section 5 also includes four practice-based interviews.

In all sections cross-referencing information runs across the bottom of the spread. This indicates where to find related and alternative approaches, and highlights glossary entries that are of interest.

Everyone has baggage that informs their thinking. So, just as politicians have to declare an interest, I thought it would be useful to include something of my history.

I am British. I was born in 1962, the only child of parents who were both designers. We three talk a great deal, about everything.

Two aspects of life that have preoccupied me since I was a child are what it means to be 'good' and the question of death. I went to a Catholic convent, so it's not hard to see that there is a correlation here.

My early musings about morality have now morphed into an interest in ethics and politics that is independent of religious belief as I do not believe that one is a prerequisite of the other.

I am a graphic designer who also writes about the subject. I consider myself liberal in my attitudes. I believe in tolerance, and resist heavily the present preoccupation with 'evil' – it is reductive and belies the complexity of morality and ethics. I don't consider cynicism to be a mark of sophistication. I may be naïvely idealistic, but I see this as a sincere and optimistic state of being.

I thought graphic design was worth doing partly because I saw it as a political activity. I came to this conclusion as a student, having been inspired by just a few texts. One was this very short piece written by the American typographer Beatrice Warde. It adorned the walls of many printers and typesetters right through to the 1980s, when I was a student. Its almost devotional language expresses a message of inclusiveness and it acts as a reminder to all those multitudes involved in print, and now visual communication, that each plays a part in the transmission of knowledge and ideas; one of the most vital human activities imaginable.

Beatrice Warde
This is a printing office
First published in 1932
as a broadsheet by the
typefounders Monotype.

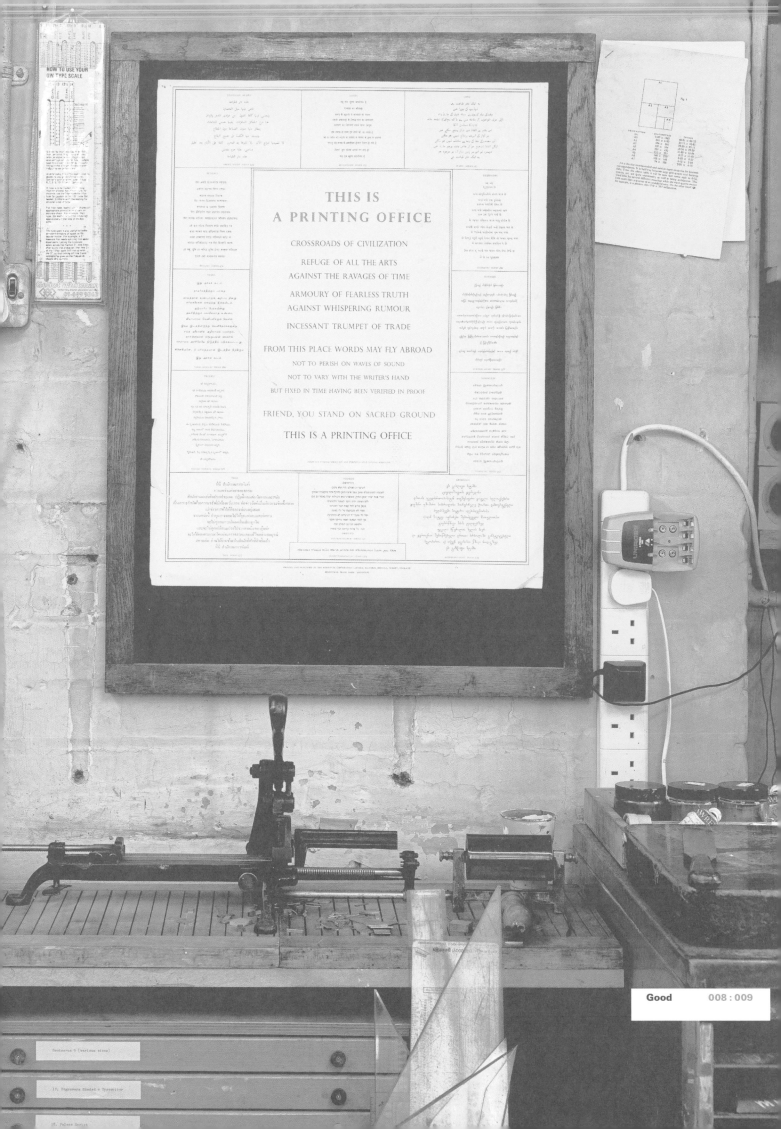

Some useful definitions

Ethics [noun]
Moral philosophy
Moral principles

Ethical [adjective]
Relating to morals
Morally correct

Moral [adjective]
Concerned with goodness or badness of human character or behaviour,
or with the distinction between right and wrong

Morals [noun]
Moral behaviour

Good [adjective]
Having the right or desired qualities
Efficient, competent, reliable
Kind, morally excellent, virtuous, charitable, well-behaved, enjoyable, beneficial
Right, proper, expedient
Attractive

Good [noun]
That which is good; what is beneficial or morally right

Right [adjective]
Just, morally or socially correct

Right [noun]
That which is morally or socially correct or just, fair treatment

All definitions taken from
The Oxford Compact English Dictionary

Good isn't...

...a showcase book because easily assimilated projects that are high on visual impact are not necessarily examples of ethical graphic design.

...a philosophy book, nor is it a theology book or a political treatise, but it does draw on all these subjects for its ideas.

...prescriptive because it would be a denial of the complexity of the subject if this were a how-to-do or what-to-think book.

...condemning because although it's important to establish ethical codes of practice, it's not easy to apply them consistently.

...evangelical because there are lots of different versions of good.

...sanctimonious because that will just make you want to be bad.

Good is...

...about ideas. Not 'design ideas', but life ideas. Please give them time. Sit in a comfortable chair, with a favourite drink and an expansive view and contemplate a little. You will find there are many rewarding detours on the way... Why am I here? Can I make a difference? Am I the centre of the universe?

...good/bad
egocentric/altruistic
vilify/glorify
collective/individual
add/subtract
monologue/dialogue
spiritual/secular
artificiality/authenticity
economical/luxurious
liberty/restraint
sanguine/doubtful
quiet/loud
on cloud nine/down in the dumps
close/open
straightforward/hazy
well-to-do/hard up
snuff out/ignite
cautious/adventurous
needy/independent
zealous/chilled
in the moment/miles away
inclusive/exclusive
prohibit/sanction
live and let live/censure
distil/prettify
reason/emotion
ordinary/magical
keen/subdued
inquisitive/blithe
meticulous/happy-go-lucky
invigorate/pacify
radiate/concentrate
right/wrong...

In the recent BBC comedy series How to Start your own Country, Danny Wallace tried to establish his East London flat as a separate country called Lovely. In this charming and naïve ruse, we were invited to consider how many of the structures that we either take for granted, or simply don't understand, actually work. Along the way, Pentagram designed him a flag, the Bank of England gave advice on currency and a cardinal at the Vatican advised on morality and rules. 'You can't improve on the Ten Commandments' said the cardinal, but back in London, Wallace decided he could simplify the whole thing: 'be good' – that's the only rule you need.

This sounds simple, but is there a shared understanding of what 'being good' means? Without one it's hard to know if this would make the world lovely. The philosopher GE Moore said that a precursor to defining good conduct is to consider what is meant by 'good' in general:

…if we can arrive at any certainty about this, it will be much easier to settle the question of good conduct; for we all know pretty well what conduct is. This, then, is our first question: What is good? and What is bad? and to the discussion of this question (or these questions) I give the name ethics…[1]

The subject of this book is ethics in a particular context: the activity of design, and specifically graphic design. The intention is to raise consciousness of ethical issues and fuel a debate about ethical graphic design practice. Ethics is a big subject – having narrowed down the territory a bit it is still impossible to provide incontrovertible answers to the complex problems posed.

Coupling ethics with graphic design might seem slightly absurd – it's just a job after all. Without indulging in self-importance or making inflated claims, it is crucial to remember that graphic design is a social activity – by its very nature it affects lots of people and with this comes a responsibility.

Beyond its immediate function, design has an effect upon any person who sees or handles it. If the function is to promote a product, service or idea, then the client will expect the effect of the design to be as wide and deep as possible. The impact can be positive or negative. Some individuals will be pleased by our design or may learn something from it. Others will be incensed at what they perceive to be wasteful and destructive of both the physical environment and the mental health of a largely captive audience. The important thing to remember is that the content of our work and the form it is given have repercussions.

What do we mean when we say a piece of design work is 'good'? Is it something to do with the talent of the designer (perhaps), catching the zeitgeist (definitely), following fashion (too often), or maybe being something of beauty (whatever that means)?

We frequently only point to the formal qualities of work when praising its excellence, but these do not exist in isolation. We should consider the needs of the client, the nature of the brief, the intended audience and budgetary limitations, and the constraints on time. The successful function of our work is often grudgingly included as a contributory factor in making it a 'good' design, but to evaluate design without examining function produces meaningless criticism.

In giving any piece of graphic work the accolade 'good', we should also go beyond its artistic and functional merits and ask questions about its 'goodness' in the wider social context. Does it contribute visually to the world in which we live? Is the message totally concerned with the product or service offered? Is the product or service entirely beneficial, or could it be harmful in any way? Is the design efficient in its use of materials and production techniques, and can it be disposed of or recycled without causing harm or involving great cost? Were the producers treated fairly and given proper recompense for the skill and effort provided? These and many other questions should be part of a designer's concerns. We are at the centre of an extensive web of ideas and actions, without which the design would not materialise. Many of these matters fall within the province of ethics or morals, and therefore have philosophical overtones.

The focus of Good

Philosophy is the starting point for this book. The practically-orientated problem-solving designer might worry that this is too abstract. Bertrand Russell wittily described philosophers as interested in defining questions but not answering them:

These philosophers remind me of the shopkeeper of whom I once asked the shortest way to Winchester. He called to a man in the back premises:

'Gentleman wants to know the shortest way to Winchester.'
'Winchester?' an unseen voice replied.
'Aye.'
'Way to Winchester?'
'Aye.'
'Shortest way?'
'Aye.'
'Dunno.'

He wanted to get the nature of the question clear, but took no interest in answering it.[2]

However, this book demonstrates that moral philosophy has absolute relevance to design practice.

Good starts with a brief historical survey of the increase in freedom, and therefore responsibility, of the artist, craftsperson and then designer. Section 2 presents philosophy, theology, politics and the law as the starting point to ethical investigation. Section 3 tests these notions in relation to graphic design. All three sections are focused on theory.

The last two sections of the book are practice-based. Section 4 is focused on what designers think about ethical design issues and Section 5 on how practice might change in the light of applying ethical ideas. Many of the ethical dilemmas designers face are the result of design being a commercial enterprise. The main focus of this book is therefore design in this context rather than as a voluntary activity or as a form of agit-prop. The work presented is not always ethical and neither are all the opinions expressed.

Is Good an ethical book?

Good is certainly ethical in intention, but only to an extent in outcome. Everyone involved has been motivated to share knowledge openly and put ethics on the design agenda. The content has been thoughtfully conceived to reflect the mixed views of a diverse set of contributors: men and women, young and old, from different backgrounds and cultures. The contributors have explored the issues with fairness and objectivity. Access to ideas has been at the forefront of everyone's mind.

Despite time pressures, everyone has been considerate to each other – polite, thoughtful, open and supportive. Fees have been paid promptly by the publisher and as staged payments throughout the process. Contributions have been acknowledged and credited.

Publishing offers lots of creative opportunities. However, the desirability of the work can mean there is minor exploitation. Fees do not match the time taken by contributors. That said, publishing is a risky business that involves investment upfront, so publishers are understandably mindful of outlay relative to projected sales.

Hopefully, the design of Good will give pleasure. The intention has been to make what could be a rather daunting subject visually engaging and therefore more accessible and appropriate for its intended audience. However, Good is not accessible to all. It does not use large print for example, although a pdf version using a reduced colour palette is available to be output at larger sizes.

Some sections of the book are printed in only one or two colours to demonstrate the visual richness of using fewer colours. The paper is recycled. However, Good was printed in the Far East where waste disposal and employment regulations are not necessarily as easy to monitor as they are within the EU, for example. This necessitated some use of air freight, although bulk transport has been by sea.

So, Good is ethical and unethical. Conflicting objectives make publishing ethically fraught. We want books that are accessible, educative and visually rich or striking. We also want them to be cheap. Under the present system, ethical compromise in making mass-produced books is almost inevitable. Responsibility lies with us all. Good asks, will change be forced upon us if we don't change first?

A positive message

This sounds rather gloomy, but it's not. Ethics is relatively unexplored territory within graphic design – the overall objective of this book is to encourage enquiry, which hopefully is a prerequisite to change.

As with many other professions, graphic design rarely presents us with huge ethical dilemmas. However, graphic design is part of the fabric of the society in which we live – even what may seem like small design decisions affect other people and reveal something of a designer's broader approach to life. In writing and researching Good it became clear that designers are aware of this responsibility, and are considering ethics in their work, but many feel confused about the relationship between professional and personal ethics, and feel too constrained by circumstance to have the 'change of heart' that Ken Garland refers to in Section 5. It seems that designers have accepted a disempowered position. The positive message of this book, however, is that each individual action matters. So, whether it is being thoughtful about what we buy, taking time to vote or spending a few extra moments in friendly conversation with a printer, it is possible to make a difference.

Good is about what we do, why we do it and most importantly whether it is worth doing. To arrive at a hard and fast set of ethical rules is at this stage perhaps too reductive and judgemental, but some kind of consensus about what being an ethical graphic designer really means is beginning to emerge.

[1]
GE Moore
Principia Ethica
1903

[2]
Bertrand Russell
Portraits from Memory
1956

Good:
An introduction to ethics in graphic design
Section 1: Making good/a brief history
Ray Roberts +
Sophia Gibb picture research /Dave Shaw photography

In all its many guises, visual art has long been the agent of moral and ethical thought. This pinboard's apparently random selection of art and design demonstrates clearly how with greater freedom, practitioners have exercised responsibility in the use of their skills.

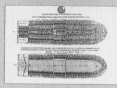

This is a brief and compressed look at the historical background to increasing ethical awareness in graphic design. It is biased towards developments in the West, partly because trade by sea, the result of European exploration, and western scientific advances were eventually the catalysts for mass manufacturing and the advent of graphic design as we know it.

Much of what this section charts is the changing role of 'artists' and then 'designers', so these terms need to be examined. Remaining evidence tells us that most people who were engaged in forms of artistic activity in the distant past trained and worked as craftspeople. They produced two- or three-dimensional artefacts, ranging from painted images to sculptures, pots, jewellery, furniture and a host of other objects for daily use. Much of this work was figurative, and took the form of illustration concerned with belief systems and the organisation of society. Other work was purely decorative or strictly functional. The current notion of the 'fine artist' as someone expressing a personal reaction to life, or exploring his or her own imaginative experiences, did not exist.

Nearer to our own time, fine artists began to set their own problems for solution and were no longer commissioned by others. The present-day designer is generally in a mid-way position between craftsperson and artist. Work is commissioned – the problems are generally given by a client – but the designer is expected to imbue the resulting solutions with an individual quality that is both appropriate to the subject and satisfying to the client.

For the sake of simplicity, for most of this section the term 'artist' is used when referring to the maker of artefacts. If there is any one theme that this section follows historically, it is that as societies have moved towards greater freedom of expression artists of all kinds have emerged as named individuals, valued for their personal contribution, but with increased responsibility for the public effect of their work. With this growing involvement in the complex weave of society, the ethical dimension of artists' work has become more powerfully evident.

for thoughts on...

→ 043
**Anthony Grayling
on freedom of expression**

→ 092
Taking responsibility

→ 116
**Michael Marriott
on artists and designers**

→ 022
Examples

Early civilisation

Since mankind first settled in organised groups, societies developed degrees of specialisation in producing the necessities of life. Artists were regarded as skilled people who could be used to support, illustrate and document visually the authority of those in power. This power might be military or political, but art nearly always reflected the higher and mystical guidance of the gods. Early societies were hierarchical and stratified, with slavery as a base. The majority of artists developed their skills as apprentices to a master, whose knowledge included the making of necessary tools and materials, and an understanding of the prevailing iconography.

For example, the civilisation of ancient Egypt extended over several millennia and expressed its rigid structures in a highly formalised manner. Sculpture was mainly static and contained vertically within its basic floor space, while painted work on flat surfaces was two-dimensional. Subject matter consisted mainly of images of the kings and queens and their exploits, the major and minor gods, and everyday rituals and activities. As beautiful as much of this work is, the effect is of formal stiffness, heavy with symbolism. Artists were controlled by priestly classes, whose interests centred on the promotion of the gods and links between those deities and the kingdom's rulers.

For a brief period in the reign of Akhenaten, who ruled between 1353–36 BC approximately, a remarkable diversion occurred. Worship was concentrated on a single god, the Aten or sun disc, and Akhenaten encouraged artists to portray himself and his queen, Nefertiti, as human beings rather than demi-gods. They are shown hand in hand, playing with their children and venturing out together in their chariot. Given the opportunity, artists revealed an ability to bring greater naturalism and freedom into their images, together with an awareness of space. This change of direction was short-lived and after the passing of Akhenaten, Egyptian art returned to its previously controlled formality.

To a great extent, this situation continued in the evolving West into the Middle Ages. The balance between religion and politics altered from time to time, but artists had to serve the prevailing belief system. An artist's ability to make personal comment, or feel responsibility, was extremely limited. Even the twentieth century showed that forceful dictatorships could repress art forms considered to be decadent or critical.

Classical societies

The growth of less rigid early societies, such as those of classical Greece and Rome, allowed more self-awareness for individuals and permitted some upward movement on grounds of merit. With the huge advantage of a simply written phonetic alphabet, more people could read and write and therefore contribute to the exchange and recording of ideas. What we know as philosophy and philosophic method had their origins in this era, when the deep concerns we still have about our beginnings and purpose were subjected to serious debate embracing ethics, morals, logic, science, psychology and literature. Secular thought ran alongside religion, and the arts became part of the spirit of enquiry. We know the names of individual artists such as Phidias, Praxiteles and Apelles, the favourite painter of Alexander the Great. Subject matter was legendary or historical, but Hellenistic art also pursued ideas about form and proportion that still exert influence today.

The small city states of ancient Greece experimented with forms of democracy, but neither this, nor the intellectual enquiries of its thinkers, stopped quarrelling and warfare between them. The growing empire of Rome absorbed these fractious states, but their culture came to permeate Roman thought and art, and was therefore transmitted throughout the empire. The Roman language, Latin, and Roman writing became the channels for Greco-Roman culture, and remained so long after their empire vanished.

The art of Rome was used partly as an instrument of propaganda, to impress and overawe its peoples. Like Grecian art, its themes included military exploits, legends and the lives of the gods. Interestingly, despite the benefits of Roman rule, opposition was felt at many levels and was expressed in scratched graffiti on public walls by disaffected slaves. Among such scratchings are those from the second century AD, which mark a momentous event for the Roman empire, the coming of Christianity. At first repressed and treated with violence, Christianity became an underground protest movement with its art drawn on tunnel walls. Eventually, Rome became Christianised and the religion spread throughout its empire. The iconography of Christianity developed gradually, and the narratives of the Bible became the subject matter of written books and wall paintings.

Glossary of ethical thought

→ 067, 068
Platonism
Aristotelianism
Epicureanism
Stoicism

1 2 3
4 5 6

1
**King Akhenaten
and Queen Nefertiti**
creator unknown
c1345 BC
One of a small number
of surviving images, this
depicts King Akhenaten
and his Queen Nefertiti with
their children. They are
shown informally, as human
beings kissing and touching,
within a truly flowing
design cut into limestone in
shallow relief. The sculptor
demonstrates skills and
understanding that were
not encouraged in the
preceding or following art
of ancient Egypt.

2
Illustration of tiles
creator and date of
tiles unknown
illustration by Owen Jones
mid-nineteenth century
The wonderful richness and
abstract invention of Islamic art
are demonstrated in these
tiles from the Alhambra Palace
in Granada, Spain. While
not permitted to depict living
beings, artists invented
a paraphrase of the natural
world in decorative symbols.
Religious restriction spurred
individual creativity.

3
**Leonardo da Vinci
The Virgin of the Rocks**
c1508
This mysterious yet humane
image is very different from
the multitude of depictions
of the Madonna and Child
from the early Middle Ages,
as beautiful as many
of those were. Warmth of
feeling, with grace of design,
make this a powerful and
memorable realisation,
enhanced by a hint of the
surreal. This painting
has become a personal
statement rather than a
hierarchical image.

4
Statue of Buddha
creator and date unknown
This statue was in the Wat
Mahathat, the largest temple in
the city of Sukhothai, the capital
of the Sukhothai kingdom of
Thailand from the thirteenth to
the fifteenth century. The inward
and contemplative nature of
Buddhism gives images of the
Buddha a timeless quality
essential to this system of
belief. Radical change is not
functional.

7

5
Misericord
creator and date unknown
Typical of the half-hidden
carvings found in medieval
churches, this underside of a
misericord in St George's
Chapel, Windsor, England
satirises the clergy by showing
a devil pushing three monks
into the mouth of hell. This
is the underside of the art
used as Christian propaganda
elsewhere in a church.

6
Pieter de Hooch
A Woman Peeling Apples
1663
De Hooch was one of many
Dutch painters who recorded
their world of middle-class
life in the seventeenth century.
Trade in goods and raw
materials with the known
world, opened up by sea,
brought considerable wealth
and comfort into the lives of
a growing part of the populace,
shown in the furniture, textiles,
clothes, interior design and
domestic architecture. Here are
the beginnings of modern life.

7
Joseph Wright of Derby
The Orrery
exhibited 1766
Wright, like many artists of
the late Enlightenment, was
fascinated by current scientific
and industrial developments.
Thinkers promoted reason
and rationality as guiding
principles, and the advances of
industrialisation were seen as
exciting and liberating, the start
of a revolution in the way life
would be lived. Religion was
challenged by new discoveries
and internal dissent.

Art and religion

With the collapse of the Roman Empire during the fifth century AD there followed the so-called Dark Ages, when dissent and strife within Europe led to the loss of much Roman technology and technical skills. However, the Christian church adopted much of the useful knowledge it found in existing written texts. Manuscripts were kept within the growing number of monasteries and these became the libraries and schools of the church, where theology and much secular knowledge were defended, nurtured and transmitted. The artistic output of the time was also created largely within the monasteries, including fine manuscript books that were mainly liturgical, alongside copies of earlier classical texts seen as useful and acceptable to the new beliefs.

Artists working in the early to late Middle Ages would have been subject to the will of the church, with its view of good and evil and the need for punishment of wrongdoing. Major subjects were the biblical narratives or the lives of Christ and the saints. The audience for such work was mainly illiterate, and in wall paintings a controlled iconography was essential for the clear delivery of the Christian message. A typical subject, found in countless versions from larger-than-life murals and sculpture, to exquisite miniatures carved in ivory, or painted on the vellum pages of books, was the image of the Virgin and Child. These obeyed rules governing symbolic content, use of colour and limitations of pose. The guild system, governing working methods, payment, quality and behaviour, expressed a limited corporate view of 'ethics', but the artists who made these images were probably driven by personal conviction, spiced with a dash of fear of those who commissioned the work. What marked out one representation from another was the quality of the interpretation. There were, however, opportunities for personal expression in medieval art. The borders of illuminated manuscripts and half-hidden architectural corners, are full of amusing and sometimes satirical imagery.

In common with Christianity, all belief systems and religions, such as Buddhism and Islam, seek to exert control upon their adherents, limiting what is acceptable in life and art. For example, strict Islamic law forbids the depiction of living beings. This gives artists an impulsion to develop powerful and decorative abstract art, which reflects the qualities of the visible world without visual imitation. Buddhism has many variations and has been followed in countries with different cultures, but its essential emphasis on the contemplative life has meant that its central figure, the Buddha, should express a timeless inward quality, unchanging in the face of change.

Towards a modern world

In Europe during the later Middle Ages and the early Renaissance, a new social class, accruing wealth from trade and banking, became politically important. To establish its status, it commissioned buildings and works of art for public use or display, and for private contemplation. Religious subjects were still important, but scenes from the life of Christ or the saints sometimes included portraits of the commissioning individual or his family, making the picture a sort of passport to the heavenly life. This fusion of the secular and religious forced new compromises on artists.

The church still used artists, but their personal interpretation of subject matter became more highly valued. The Sistine Chapel ceiling and The Virgin of the Rocks, for example, show the power of great artists in making these basic tales so vivid. It was broadly acknowledged that art could help shape society, but with this came artists' realisation that they had to move with extreme care. Religious and political divisions also forced the taking of sides. Portraits of the powerful assumed much greater importance, with figures placed against or among their possessions. Artists began using their skills to reveal something of the inner life, as well as the appearance of the sitter, but were also under pressure to flatter. Truth, half-truth, and untruth were there to test the artist in new ways: visual editing became a required skill.

During the Renaissance, scientific method began to be used in widening understanding of how the world works. Many artists, most notably Leonardo da Vinci, combined artistic skills and scientific techniques to probe the nature of things. An uneasy conflict between religion and science led to many acts of suppression and brutality, making artists' lives sometimes precarious.

for thoughts on...

→ 052
**Richard Holloway
on religion and ethics**

→ 133
**Chris de Bode
on truth**

→ 164–167
**The global and
business context
to design**

→ 022, 023, 026, 027
Examples

This ferment of ideas and activity then received an unprecedented boost with the invention of printing using movable type. From the mid-fifteenth century onwards, Gutenberg's innovations heralded the easy cross-fertilisation of ideas and the possibility of universal literacy. Seen as a blessing by some and as a threat to social stability by others, printing was fundamental to the rapid spread and democratisation of knowledge. It played its part in the rise of Protestantism, splitting the Christian faith, followed by further subdivisions into nonconformism. Similarly, the literature of science gave impetus to new thinking. Books in small formats were available cheaply, their texts made more effective by the use of engraved illustration. Combined words and images pointed the way to future graphic design.

Science and trade

During the eighteenth century, discoveries in optics and astronomy, together with technological developments in timekeeping, allied to sensitive engraving techniques, made navigational maps more accurate and reliable. To some extent this marked the beginning of the globalisation of today, as trading by sea increased between the East and West, and the merchant classes of seafaring nations became wealthier. Artists depicted the houses, gardens and daily life of these new middle classes, surrounded by their collections of fine objects from around the world.

By the mid-eighteenth century the Industrial Revolution was underway in northern Europe, with new inventions replacing handwork with machine production. Many people moved from the countryside to the growing towns in search of a better life. Early experiments in popular education led to increased literacy, and the printing and publishing industries responded with news sheets, pamphlets, journals and prints covering many aspects of daily life.

Initially, industrialisation, which resulted from scientific discovery, was seen as an exciting adventure with dramatic visual consequences. Artists recorded laboratory experiments and changing landscapes, which were engraved as popular prints or magazine illustrations.

With industrialisation, mass communication became progressively easier, so that awareness of distant events and their effects became part of public consciousness. Artists saw that they had a role beyond reinforcing the status quo or simply documenting life and its changes. Concern for others began to extend beyond the next village, and governments were forced to become more responsive. Public agitation helped, for example, in ending the notorious British slave trade in 1807, while throughout the nineteenth century pressure increased to improve the lives of the impoverished and oppressed.

The benefits of industrial life were balanced by a darker side, with overcrowded cities, disease and poverty being the daily lot of thousands of people. Through the late eighteenth century to the mid-nineteenth century artists like Goya, Hogarth, Blake, Gillray, Cruikshank, Doré and Daumier used the artist's print to reveal and attack many public abuses, employing satire as a potent weapon. Some of the most effective onslaughts on entrenched ideas were by word and image in combination, with writers such as Dickens taking a lead.

In a partial reaction against the dehumanising results of industrial methods, the artist and thinker William Morris attempted to fuse creation and production in the making of things. He argued that the worker should be responsible for the way a product looked and functioned, as well as the way it was made, and advocated a return to some aspects of craft manufacture. Morris's design approach and ideas about the dignity of work still have an influence on modern design philosophy, but in reality his theories could not satisfy the needs of a modern population and his project failed economically.

Glossary of ethical thought

→ 066
Buddhism
Confucianism

→ 068, 069
Christian ethics
Utilitarianism
Kantian ethics

8

8
Gustave Doré
London 1872
1872
The darker side of industrial
growth, with overcrowding,
insanitary housing and chaotic
city travel, is shown in this
reaction to London by Doré.
Yet he also found the ebullient
spirit of the city dweller worthy
of note. His drawings raised
awareness and in so doing
helped Mayhew and others
who sought improvements
through planning and
better medical services.

9
Engraving illustrating
the stowage of slaves
The Abolitionist League
1789
This horrifying engraving
gains strength from its
apparently diagrammatic
approach. The simple
presentation of factual
inhumanity made a great
contribution towards the
campaign for the abolition
of the British slave trade.
Some 420 souls, crammed
into minimal space on small
ships, left nothing to the
imagination. This is powerful,
apposite graphic design,
without illusions.

10
James Gillray
The plum-pudding in danger
published 1805
Gillray was one of numerous
artists who took advantage
of the growing printing
and publishing trades to
attack prevailing social
structures. These cartoons
were often harsh, illustrating
the ineffective, self-seeking
weakness of the powerful
and therefore arousing
public anger. As a channel
for protest and change, the
modern political cartoon
is still important and useful.

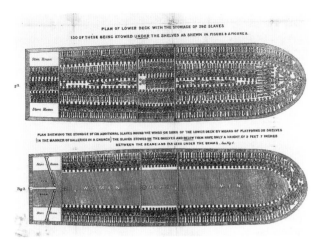

9 10
11 12 13

11
William Morris & Co
Sussex chair, with arms
made c1875–1900
This chair designed by
Morris typifies his strengths
and weaknesses. Although he
sought to provide things of
use and beauty for everybody,
Morris's emphasis on craft-
based manufacture meant his
designs were expensive and
therefore only available to the
fashionably rich.

12
Programme cover,
National American Women's
Suffrage Association
March 1913
It is clear from the earliest
records that civilisations have
mostly regarded women as
inferior, to be repressed and
protected. The forces unleashed
by the Enlightenment and the
demands of the Industrial
Revolution led inevitably to the
emancipation of women. The
fight was long and hard, with
the right to vote coming to
many advanced democracies
only in the twentieth century.
Here is just one of many
graphic expressions of protest.

13
Maurice Becker
Cover, The Masses, entitled
Whom the Gods would
Destroy They First Make Mad
September 1914
This cover illustrates that even
early in the First World War
there was criticism and a desire
for pacifist action against
the coming disaster. The issues
were hard to resolve and
always inconclusive. The
struggle to achieve satisfactory
solutions through rational
discussion rather than violence
is with us still, raising hard,
ethical problems.

The responsive and responsible designer

The political strains and appalling misjudgements that led up to the First World War and its aftermath revealed the turmoil of forces underlying modern life: industrial, economic, political and social. Design theorists felt that old ways of thinking and doing could not be stretched to contain these forces: new mental and physical structures were needed.

This led in part to artists examining their role in society. Were they best used by servicing commerce and, hopefully, increasing wealth for the many – or by producing political propaganda that advocated social upheaval and change?

The arrival of graphic design as a distinct practice was in large part the result of the Industrial Revolution. Production was no longer a local affair, so by the late nineteenth century advertising had become an industry in its own right, using artists of all kinds, supported by a host of engravers and the printing industry. Potential clients were expanding their markets across national borders, raising capital internationally, and establishing brand names. The skills of artists and writers were harnessed by agencies to help companies fix their brands in the public mind. By the early 1920s some art schools offered courses in 'commercial art'.

Running concurrently with this, governments used promotional material for public pronouncements and propaganda, and politically motivated groups, like the British and American suffragettes, used visual communication powerfully to advocate their cause. Political divisions between democratic states and corporate states were also expressed in what we would now define as graphic design.

The Arts and Crafts Movement, which had grown out of Morris's ideas, was behind late nineteenth century attempts to improve living conditions through publicly-owned housing. These ideas were absorbed into the much more radical approaches to modern living created in Europe, especially in Russia and Germany. Among design schools, the German Bauhaus was most notable in this regard. The school aimed to make a better world through careful design at all levels. It advocated using craft skills to create products that could be mass-produced to make modern and effective design available to all. The Bauhaus was allied politically with the Left. When the Nazis rose to power in the 1930s the school was closed down, but members who could do so left Germany, emigrating to freer parts of the West and thereby spreading Bauhaus ideals.

During the Second World War, all participating states required strong communication between governments and the governed. This encouraged graphic design to evolve in the creative and technical senses. With the return of peace, there was a general determination that the pre-war economic conditions suffered by millions, together with war itself, would never occur again. The practice of graphic design was conditioned by these feelings. Many designers became openly political and questioned the intentions of their clients, public or private.

By the 1960s, graphic design had become a subject of serious study in art schools, supported by various professional bodies in many countries. With so-called economies of scale, industries had become more powerful – with companies operating internationally. Brands were recognised worldwide through symbols and logotypes, demonstrating much greater awareness of the importance of design. Apart from those who were directly employed, designers worked individually or formed larger groups that could offer a complete service, covering all aspects of a company's visual presentation. Individual designers often worked for public bodies or government agencies, while larger group practices served business corporations. At that time, awareness of 'ethics' in the way that life was conducted had become a topic for discussion, with a general feeling that public bodies were less suspect than large private companies.

for thoughts on...

→ 062
Delyth Morgan
on design and politics

→ 110
Designers as citizens
of the world

→ 137
Sheila Levrant de Bretteville
on inclusion

→ 030, 031
Examples

Throughout the last 30 years graphic design has become part of the social landscape, projecting ideas about the nature of 'the good life'. It has also had growing overtones of glamour, with links to the fashion industry and popular culture. Objects are now given appeal by the prefix 'designer': designer shirts, designer bags and so on.

Many art students, who might otherwise have studied fine art, have chosen design instead, believing that it will provide creative freedom plus an ensured income. But the allure of perceived self-expression has often diverted attention from the more mundane, but absolutely necessary, importance of content.

Sophisticated graphics promote ever widening ranges of products and services seen as essential to human fulfilment. But presentation has dominated over information, and despite notable exceptions, even the serious information-based publicity of many charitable organisations has succumbed to sugar-coated enticement.

The developments in corporate business and large scale government have made questions of ethics even more crucial. A simple answer to a multitude of problems is not possible, especially since the other great post-war divide between democratic free-market states and centrally-controlled economies has now collapsed. We face a looming uncertainty over the future of our planet, which will probably alter radically the ways in which we produce, trade, and relate to each other across the globe. Survival will almost certainly force us away from our concern with passing novelty.

Graphic design is a potent tool for good or bad, as we can see in war propaganda or political promotion. Truth is an easy victim of power. All the awareness and understanding we now possess have failed to eliminate cruelty, oppression and war. Great wrongs have still to be righted on many fronts in the world community. Electronic communication has now almost destroyed distance and time, so that we have little excuse for not being aware of the world's ills. Practically every decision we make as designers has an ethical dimension, requiring us all to 'balance the forces' in our own small way as responsible individuals.

Glossary of ethical thought

14 15
16 17 18

14
Viktor Klimaschin
Poster, USSR Agricultural
Exhibition
dated 1939
Early Communist Russian
political art was often very
advanced graphically. However,
by the 1930s populism and
social realism had come to
portray life falsely as a series
of heroic victories over natural
and industrial difficulties –
the result of successful five-year
plans. The collosal yet perfect
human image typifies visual
propaganda of all kinds.

15
Ludwig Mies van der Rohe
Weissenhof settlement
apartment houses, Stuttgart
built 1927
Ideas from the Bauhaus
influenced much continental
public housing in the decades
before the Second World War.
Modern construction methods
were used to provide humane
living spaces supported by high
quality services. These were
expressed through clean
rectangular external lines.
Landscaping was seen as part
of the total scheme, flowing
around the structures.

16
Abram Games
Poster, Use of Your Talk
1941
During war, communication
by government to people is
vital. Of numerous forceful
posters by Games, this makes
the point that careless talk
about knowledge gained in any
occupation could be turned
against the cause. Idle words
become a death-dealing
bayonet. This is an example
of localised ethics.

17
Ken Garland
Cover, First Things First
manifesto
1964
This manifesto was a plea for
designers and photographers
to use their skills responsibly,
rather than in the promotion
of trivia from pet food to
cosmetics. The intention
was serious and supported
by 21 leading practitioners;
but the issues were not simple
or clear-cut and were difficult
to resolve in a relatively free
society. They remain relevant
but contentious, as witnessed
in the publication of a second,
revised manifesto in 2000.

GREENPEACE

Shelter

19

20

18
Nick Ut
June 1972
This unforgettable photograph illustrates self-inflicted horror, in which a plane from South Vietnam accidentally dropped flaming napalm on its own troops and many civilians during the Vietnam War. This and other portrayals of foul war must surely strengthen opposition to violence. The badly burnt girl at the centre did survive. Nick Ut, the photographer, was honoured in 2006 for his work with Associated Press.

19
Milton Glaser
World Health Organization
AIDS symbol
1987
Greenpeace logo
designer and date unknown
Johnson Banks
Shelter logo
2004
Graphic design today includes the establishment of brands on behalf of companies and their products. The importance of easy visual recognition has now been acknowledged by many non-profit organisations, as seen here.

20
Alan Kitching
Why Iraq? Why Now?
2003
A hard-hitting typographic design using old and worn wood type to emphasise the urgency of its message on the eve of a new war. This appeared as a newspaper advertisement bearing the names of scores of influential supporters. Here words are the image. By removing the list of names at its base it was utilised as a placard for participants in the next day's global anti-war rallies.

As this brief historical survey illustrates, visual art has long been the agent of moral and ethical thought. It can persuade, educate or control. Patrons have commissioned to great effect while artists have deliberated about the appropriate use of their skills.

Graphic design is a relatively new practice – it is the response to changing needs resulting from industrialisation, and scientific and technological development. Although the abundance and nature of much design work is a direct reflection of its time, this does not mean that designers are not accountable. The unifying premise of this section is that as individual freedom has increased so has individual responsibility. Artists, and now designers, are therefore increasingly called upon to question the ethical dimension of their work.

Good:
An introduction to ethics in graphic design
Section 2: Approaching good/a survey of theory
Lucienne Roberts +
Anthony Grayling/Jacqueline Roach/
Richard Holloway/Delyth Morgan/
Naomi Goulder/Frederik Willemarck/
Dave Shaw photography

Anthony Grayling is Professor of Philosophy at Birkbeck College, University of London, and a Supernumary Fellow of St Anne's College, Oxford, England. His broad philosophical interests include the examination of how we might define and determine fundamental concepts such as truth, happiness and guilt. Widely published, he has made philosophy relevant to everyday life through his many books, broadcasts and essays, including his Last Word column in the Guardian newspaper. He was the Honorary Secretary of the Aristotelian Society and is a past Chairman of June Fourth, a group concerned with human rights in China. Grayling is a Fellow of the World Economic Forum, and a member of its C-100 group on relations between the West and the Islamic world. He is a Fellow of the Royal Society of Arts, and is a previous Booker Prize judge. [British, born 1949]

LR
The philosophy section in the nearest bookshop to the University of London is on the top floor and reached via the back stairs. How strange that books entitled **The Meaning of Things** and **Making Sense** should not greet one at the front door. Although they can't give a definitive answer, it is reassuring not to be alone in asking the question. Anthony Grayling, the author of one such book, seemed just the right person to talk to for this section.

LR

Graphic designers are responsible to many
people, and the commercial aspect of
the work can distort this. Is it possible to
arrive at an ethical code of practice for
an activity like graphic design?

AG

Yes, absolutely. A code that says 'thou shalt'
and 'thou shalt not' is inflexible and fits awkwardly
with real life, which is complex and protean.
Therefore to devise an ethical code for designers,
one would do better to say: here are examples
of what a responsible and well-intentioned designer
might be like; go and do likewise. A list of strict
rules would be very difficult to observe in practice,
which is always the problem with top-down
ethics. The alternative idea of 'a way of being'
is bottom-up, which rests on individuals being
conscious of their involvement in society and
the impact they have on it.

Like everyone else, designers find themselves
in a spider's web of duties – contractual duties,
duties to clients, to stakeholders, to colleagues, to
themselves and their work, and to society at large.
It's sometimes difficult to serve everybody well
while at the same time fulfilling one's implicit duties
to society. I think it legitimate for someone to say
that they try their best, and to learn from failures.

Money can be a distorting factor in all aspects
of life and work, and therefore here too. Technically
money should be a neutral instrument that enables
things to happen. It's useful to have a coin in your
pocket to buy bread rather than a sack of coal to
be exchanged for it. But money too often becomes
an end in itself and this can distort some people's
sense of responsibility.

Normally, of course, financial exchange involves
a mutual benefit. The payer is buying a professional
service that adds value to their own endeavours.
The client has duties too – to all their stakeholders
and to society at large, just as the professional does.
These are equivalent to, and sometimes greater
than, the duties of the professionals they hire.

for thoughts on...

→ **049**
Jacqueline Roach
on professionalism

→ **094–099**
Work and happiness

→ **129**
Simon Esterson
on happiness

→ **139**
Sheila Levrant de Bretteville
on work as mutual benefit

LR

Having creative freedom brings happiness
to the designer, but what about work that may
be less personally satisfying, but helps others?
Is my happiness more important than the
happiness of everyone else?

AG

I've always thought that if you want to live a good
life, and to do good in the world, you've got to
be good to yourself. You have a responsibility
to be a good steward of your own gifts, and you've
got to take care of yourself in order to be a more
flourishing and effective person. This is something
people forget, despite its being so simple and
obvious a point.

There is a utilitarian argument that says you
have to maximise benefit for the greatest number;
so for example you would then work for (say)
charities all the time instead of doing the work
that most engages you personally. If the two
coincide that's great: for then what benefits you
individually, making you happier, more effective,
more productive, more alive and creative, is also
an outward contribution. But if one sought to be
altruistic at the expense of one's own interest
all the time, the risk is that it would eventually
undermine even one's ability to be good to others.

When you are involved in less creatively satisfying
projects, which nonetheless benefit others,
I would start by saying that you have a professional
obligation to advise your client and to express
your point of view on the basis of your experience.
So, you would say that if tackled differently there
could be a more attractive and interesting outcome.
If the client says 'no, we want it like this' then I think
you've got another professional obligation, which is
ultimately to accept the aesthetic judgement made
by the client, because it's not as if you're committing
a sin by designing a less visually interesting
leaflet (or whatever). Your moral obligation to be
professional is engaged in such cases.

Glossary of ethical thought

→ 067
Aristotelianism

→ 069
Utilitarianism

LR
I think that most designers are keen to produce useful objects that are aesthetically striking. Is there a relationship between aesthetics and ethics?

AG
There is a very important connection between them. Here we need to go back a couple of steps to be clear about these different terms. Firstly, we're using the term 'ethics' here to mean something very inclusive, something more general than we normally mean by morality. Morality is about the rights and wrongs of certain kinds of behaviour, particularly in our relationships. But our ethos is about how we live, what sort of people we are, and what kind of society we create between us. For example: it's an ethical matter what colour you paint your house, because this is about your ethos, that is, the way you live and the sort of person you are; but it's not a moral matter (unless it's such a vile colour that it really upsets your neighbours).

So, ethics is a more inclusive notion. It's about the whole quality of life. The aesthetic becomes really vital to that because to live in a social and political setting which is pleasing, enticing and attractive, and which is full of interest, detail, colour and movement increases the quality of life. Compare this to living in a Tupperware box or somewhere ugly, sleazy and broken down. Every aspect of our lives is touched constantly by considerations of the quality of our experience. So there is a deep connection between the aesthetic and the ethical for this reason.

for thoughts on...

→ 054
**Richard Holloway
on instrumental
and intrinsic goods
in the arts**

→ 096
Beauty and quality of life

→ 123
**Billie Tsien
on quiet pleasure**

→ 133
**Chris de Bode
on the power of
beautiful images**

LR
So one design responsibility is to make
the world a more beautiful place?

AG

I'd say: one design objective, wherever possible.
The concept of beauty itself is such a vexed
one, requiring answers to questions about how
you define it, whether it's subjective (a projection
of our preferences) or objective (something
pre-existing that we discover in the world). Leave
all that discussion aside for the moment and try
using the technique of finding paraphrases, other
words or expressions, for the cluster of things
you mean when you talk about beauty. Talk about
what pleases, what's enchanting, what's attractive,
what's striking, what's moving, what makes
a difference, what makes an impact: and in that
cluster of different things we will find what we
mean by beauty.

Now it would seem to me that a designer who
paid no attention to whether their work was
striking, enchanting or interesting would be failing.
So the answer to the question, 'do designers have
a responsibility to try and make the world a more
beautiful place?', is yes, whenever possible.
It fits into this broad sense of the ethical, which is
the nature and quality and meaning of a life.

Depending on whether you're fundamentally
religious or fundamentally not religious you will
take a different view of the world and human
beings. I'm not religious. Religious people say
that there are supernatural agencies that demand
that we live a certain sort of life and that it is our
response to this demand that constitutes our
spiritual life. Somebody like me, whose view is
naturalistic (that is, who thinks the world is
determined by scientific laws), will say that our
ethics must be based on facts about human
nature and the human condition, and that our
emotional and intellectual life arises from
how we are constituted.

I'm always struck by seeing people strolling in
the country, pottering about in a garden or looking
at paintings in an art gallery, because these are
spiritual exercises in this naturalistic sense. People
doing these things are in effect refreshing their
hearts and minds. Now design, which can so richly
enhance the beauty of the world, is thereby adding
to the spiritual value of the world.

Glossary of ethical thought

→ 070
Marxism

LR
Designers put a huge amount of energy
into the craft aspects of their work.
This is often almost invisible, certainly to
the client. Is it justifiable to ask a client
to pay for this?

AG

Let's consider the legendary tale of a sculptor
carefully carving the folds of cloth on the back of
a statue that is going to be placed against a wall.
Someone asks him, 'why are you spending so much
time doing that – nobody's going to see it?', to which
the sculptor replies, 'I can see it'. I think that in the
end the intrinsic value of something comes from
the individual craftsman's or artist's sense of
integrity in the production of the work. The quality
of the work is independent of considerations of
money or anything else.

That said; you asked if it is fair to charge your
client for let's say carefully spacing all the headings
in a print job. I would say absolutely yes. You
could rephrase your question by asking, can we
only charge our clients for things that they would
notice? But the fact that the letter spacing is not
noticed may well be a function of its being right.
A wonderfully eloquent and masterful lecturer
makes it look easy, makes everybody think they
themselves could just stand up and do it too.
But the people in the hall don't realise that this is
something that has been worked on, developed
and thought about. In fact when things look
easy and natural so that you don't notice the nuts
and bolts, it's because they're so well done.
If a client wants the best out of a professional he
should be ready to pay for this without hesitation.
This is all about quality of life.

LR

Everything is seen as relative so it is much harder to talk about value in design now than it used to be. Is it possible to say that by using a certain approach to a design problem you will arrive at the right answer?

AG

Let's firstly consider the extremes. One is absolutism, which says 'this is right or wrong'. Then there is the relativist position, which says everybody's judgement about whether something is right or wrong is his or her own – a kind of free-for-all. The conceptual space between them is best navigated by looking for alternative terms instead of 'good'. In the context of design, people might talk about effective, striking or accessible design. The result is a family of concepts, which are resources to explain to people what you mean when you say 'I think this is good design'.

Relativism per se just simply means that there is no way of adjudicating a difference of taste over something. You say, 'this is a piece of good design' and someone else says 'no, it's lousy'. That sort of clash is entailed in the simplest and crudest form of relativism. But most often I think when people say tastes differ, attitudes differ, preferences differ, they're not really saying this in order to bolster a crude form of relativism. They're saying it because there are indeed differences of taste, and of standards, between people in these matters: but it's not as though they can't be negotiated out of those differences.

As to finding the right solution, I would suggest that there are good ways of approaching a problem, which give you a right answer. Because, without being relativistic, the truth is that there are different good ways of doing things. A writer for example has no responsibility to tell the truth, but does have a responsibility to tell a_ truth – and the same approach applies in design.

Glossary of ethical thought

→ 073
Ethics of difference

LR
Is all graphic design, apart from information design perhaps, a form of manipulation?

AG
The word 'manipulation' is loaded. I'd say that graphic design is an aspect of rhetoric. It stems from the art of rhetoric that was developed in classical antiquity when oratory, or verbal eloquence, was the only means of conveying information, persuading people, changing their minds and putting a point of view. Nowadays, with the divergence of forms of communication, rhetoric has become a diverse thing. Design is one form of it. Whether design is used in presenting a point of view or a piece of information, it is used to get the message across in an attractive or impactful way that will get people's attention. It's in this sense that it's an extension of the rhetorical art.

That has a good and a bad side. The good side is that people must be informed and must be aware of different points of view. It's a service to people to be alerted to things and to know about them.

In looking at the bad side, we should start by understanding that in itself, design is neutral. It ceases to be neutral in the light of its content. Its value morally is in the content it portrays. Take Nazi design as an example. It is generally agreed that the Nazi regime used design to tremendous effect. On one level it was 'good' design. So, imagine that someone lands from Mars and sees the great building in Berlin commissioned by Goering for the Luftwaffe ministry. It's a fantastic bit of fascist architecture and in itself it's a rather beautiful object. However, once you are told it was put up by the Nazis and for what purpose, your value judgement is influenced by that fact. This demonstrates the tremendous difficulty in separating form and content, and emphasises the fact that the moral value of a piece of design working as a rhetorical device wholly rests in the fact that it has this content.

for thoughts on…

→ 047
**Jacqueline Roach
on the 'cab rank rule'**

→ 088–093
Deciding who to work for

→ 140
**Sheila Levrant de Bretteville
on moral superiority**

→ 181
**Violetta Boxill
on accepting a brief**

LR
Should designers only take on jobs from clients whose ethos they agree with?

AG

We live in an open, pluralistic society and with very few and rather special exceptions, like hate speech and racist speech, we like to see people put their point of view, even if we disagree with them – sometimes vehemently. We think that it's very important for our own views to be challenged and that there should be a lively and multifaceted public debate. The health of a society depends on this. We may often not like what we hear, but if we're serious about making our own contribution then we should listen to others and engage with their points.

Now, in such a society we want it to be the case not only that people can put their point of view, but that they can do this in the best possible way. We accept that somebody on the other side of the argument from us is entitled to present their case as powerfully and eloquently as they can. It's right and proper therefore that people can make use of things like advertising and the media and design to potentiate their case.

Even if you don't personally agree with your client's message, if the message is a legitimate one do you take a stand based on our own personal morality or do you act as a professional and continue to provide a service? Professional interests and obligations are perfectly legitimate, and the value of free speech and the value of alternative points of view are so great that it must surely be up to individuals to decide what moral stance they take. It is a matter of personal conscience and degree.

But all that said, it remains the case that if something were really such a serious matter for you ethically then even if it meant financial loss or other problems, the answer is very, very simple. If it really is a moral make or break issue for you, you don't do things that you don't agree with.

Jacqueline Roach **trained as
a journalist and worked at the Women's Press
before joining the National Association
of Citizens Advice Bureaux, where she was
in charge of press and publicity. In 1996
she was called to the Bar. Since becoming
a barrister she has covered a cross-section
of public law work, specialising in family
law and representing local authorities,
parents and children. Roach is involved in
running legal cases from the first court
appearance through to the final hearing and
has appeared in courts at all levels, from the
Family Proceedings Court to the High Court.
Her particular interest is in fact-finding
hearings where there is a question of serious
non-accidental injury or sexual abuse,
parents with mental illness or psychological
difficulties, or domestic violence.
[British, born 1962]**

LR
The law is one instrument we use to enforce
agreed ethical and moral values. Courtroom
dramas represent it as something heightened
and passionate, but to work effectively as
a barrister it is vital to retain objectivity and to
keep a clear eye on the overarching values of
the profession. Jacqueline Roach knows from
her time working in publicity that, rather
like barristers, graphic designers represent
clients and use a form of rhetoric to do so.
She was just the right person to consider
if that is where the parallel between the two
professions ends.

LR

The relationship between ethics, morality and the law seems obvious – it is the reinforcement of our agreed notions of good and bad, right and wrong. Is it that simple and straightforward?

JR

Yes, in that the law is about upholding agreed moralities. However, as a lawyer you don't run your practice on the basis of whether your client is a good or a bad person. The principle is that everybody deserves to be represented. My job is not to make a moral judgement about my client, or what he or she is said to have done, but to represent them to the best of my ability.

I do this on the basis of what they tell me, not on the basis of what I suspect is true or untrue. If, for instance, my client says 'I did murder that child', I can't then run their case on the basis that they didn't, because I would be misleading the court. This is what is called being 'professionally embarrassed' and I would have to withdraw from the case under these circumstances.

We do advise our clients however. So, I can say to a client, 'nobody's going to believe that, and if you want me to run your case in this way these are the consequences'. This is my duty but they can ignore my advice, in which case I continue to act on their instructions.

There are some absolutes in the law, like being innocent until proven guilty or not bringing somebody's character into evidence unless they themselves do. The principle here is that you're not trying somebody on their past, you're trying them on the basis of facts presented in relation to this one case. One has to look at evidence as probative or prejudicial, and if it's totally prejudicial or highly prejudicial but not particularly probative then it shouldn't be brought into question.

Context however is significant, as is state of mind. That's the difference between murder and manslaughter for instance. For murder you have to have planned to commit the act, but manslaughter can be an accident or there can be mitigating circumstances such as mental illness. In this way the law tries to strike a balance between intention and outcome.

The law isn't just determined by ethical principles of course. We often don't break the law in making decisions that we think are ethically dodgy – I wouldn't say wrong, who am I to say what somebody else's ethics are? But nobody can live a totally ethical life – we are yet to define it for a start.

for thoughts on...

→ 088–093
Deciding who to work for

→ 166
The business context of design

→ 189
Dan Eatock on diversity of approach

LR

Graphic designers are almost agents for their clients, so there are ethical choices about the sort of work we do. Presumably there are some jobs that you turn down on ethical grounds?

JR

As a barrister you're not allowed to say that you won't do a job because it's against your morals or ethical code. It's the 'cab rank rule' – a case comes up and you've got to take it. This goes back to my original points. The important principles are that everyone has the right to a fair trial, and that you are innocent until proven otherwise. Seen from that perspective, on what moral or ethical basis could I turn a job down?

This doesn't mean that certain chambers don't have reputations for doing particular sorts of work or for being politically more left- or right-wing. This of course will have a bearing on the kind of work they are asked to do. It may also mean being more obviously compromised at times. The Brixton Bomber, for example, was represented by a barrister from a left-wing chambers. You can see why his solicitor would have advised this – how could this have been a racially motivated attack if his brief is of this persuasion? So it's quite cynical sometimes, why people are briefed.

When it comes to graphic design, isn't it better not to walk away from jobs on ethical grounds, but to ask if there's some way that you can have influence, something you can bring? Otherwise, I would have said that the law is racist and sexist, and not had anything to do with it. Your job and mine are about influence and persuasion. A judge may well have certain views at the beginning of the case and different ones by the end. Most certainly those views are not going to be challenged if I'm not there.

This is also about prejudice. You might be pleasantly surprised working for a corporate client, certainly that's what I found at the Bar. Yes, the Bar's full of unpleasant, arrogant people who think that it's their God-given right to be there, but it's also full of really sound people. I'm not talking about their political persuasion; they're good people who are very good at what they do and want to make a positive difference.

Glossary of ethical thought

→ 066
Confucianism

→ 073
Ethics of difference

LR

It sounds as though reason, rather than emotion, has to be the determining factor in your work. Isn't it hard to remain dispassionate and not to despair of humanity?

JR

I think mine is a brutal profession because we're at the sharp end of society – somebody wants something that somebody else has got, whether it's their child or their liberty or their money. It's not conducive to kindness and humanity.

That said, just as newspaper articles about old people and the risk of mugging skew the facts, I have to remember that the people I see represent a tiny minority in society. I think that, unfortunately, given a particular set of circumstances, a lot of people do behave badly towards each other. They are in extremis and wounded, but we're all wounded in some way, so I do believe that people decide whether they're going to behave in a certain way.

I don't believe that it would be mayhem without the law. Human beings find their level, but they do like rules. They like to know where they are, how things fit into the scheme of things – that the consequence of 'x' is 'y'. Being told that anything goes can make you feel valueless. That's why the Tories do better on the big moral issues because they will say, 'this is bad and this is good', while Labour says, 'well this may be not so great and this not so good, possibly'. When people are feeling in a state of crisis they want certainty. This is why certain iniquitous societies have flourished – Nazism for example.

With regard to reason and emotion, you can't disassociate the two. It's inevitable that certain cases are emotionally charged and so we actually need the lawyers to take the heat out of it. It would be counter-productive for barristers to be emotional about their cases. Solicitors inevitably get much closer to the case than we do – we only see the client in court or if we have a conference. We don't have them coming through our doors or ringing us up constantly, telling us 'you've done this' or 'she's done that'. Solicitors do. You can see if you look through a course of correspondence of a particularly fraught case how solicitors are drawn into this emotional mess. We're there to step back from it and say, 'this is what I think and this is what the outcome will probably be'.

for thoughts on…

→ 055
Richard Holloway
on humility

→ 062
Delyth Morgan
on emotional detachment

→ 134
Chris de Bode
on coping with distress

LR

There are interesting parallels between your role as a barrister and mine as a graphic designer. We are both briefed, represent a client and use rhetoric to persuade. However, you seem to be more objective and less focused on personal gratification in your work than most designers.

JR

A judge doesn't care what I personally think, but obviously if I didn't feel personal gratification and pride in my work I wouldn't do it. There are real highs in my job. Sometimes the work is intellectually demanding and you can feel real euphoria when you win a case against the odds. But you have to ask the question, what are you getting that pleasure from? Is it from giving what you think is a really good speech based on crap, or because you really believe in your client's case and you've won?

As you say, my job requires rhetorical skill. I have been trained to use verbal language to influence messages in subtle and unsubtle ways. You use a visual language. Both bring responsibilities. Your layout, for example, can make someone read text and images quite differently.

As you know, before training as a barrister I worked in communications. A project we worked on together is a good example of what I mean: the Citizens Advice Bureau logo. We were trying to show through graphic design that the service wasn't an anachronism – only white and middle class. A by-product was that the design was great, but I think that the message that the design was giving was more important than its pure aesthetics. These had to reinforce the message so that it was communicated to the intended audience. Both would have been lost otherwise, or it would have been a vanity piece of work.

With regard to the client, in order to do my job properly I engage with their brief – I'm not just a mouthpiece for them. Ideally there is a two-way discourse. They're the client and have the final say, but there are ways in which I can influence them too.

Broadly, I get satisfaction from contributing as a professional. It would be unethical to take a client's money and then not represent them to the best of my ability. That is what I've been employed to do. If we are honest, most of us are not great thinkers and do not have a fantastically earth-shattering message to give. We are just little worker bees really, but that doesn't mean that we can't do our jobs well or contribute effectively.

Richard Holloway was Bishop of Edinburgh and Primus of the Scottish Episcopal Church until 2000. An outspoken figure and moderniser in the Anglican Church, Holloway explores theological, spiritual and ethical dilemmas in his many books, essays and broadcasts. He was Gresham Professor of Divinity in the City of London, and his appointments have included Chair of the British Medical Association Steering Group on Ethics and Genetics. He is Patron of Lesbian, Gay, Bisexual and Transgender (LGBT) Youth Scotland and has been a member of the Broadcasting Standards Commission and the Human Fertilisation and Embryology Authority. Holloway is a Fellow of the Royal Society of Edinburgh and is currently Chair of the Scottish Arts Council. At the moment he is exploring the Venezuelan system of children's and youth orchestras as a possible instrument of social transformation for those living in deprived communities in Scotland. [British, born 1933]

LR
For some time the church had a bit of a stranglehold over goodness – and badness for that matter. This historical connection means that many people unquestioningly assume that faith is a prerequisite to good behaviour, despite there often being no tangible difference between the actions of religious and non-religious people. There seemed no better person to discuss this with than former bishop Richard Holloway, author of **Godless Morality**. Holloway's work has embraced many faiths, and is characterised by tolerance and liberal values. He sees Christianity as 'an art form rather than as a body of revealed absolute truth'.

LR

Most people think there's some connection between religion and ethics, but obviously you don't have to be religious to behave well. Is there a relationship between the two?

RH

There may be a historical relationship, but I don't think it's an essential relationship. It's not absolute anyway. The Greeks invented the study of ethics, and religion was hardly mentioned. But religions, like all power groups, are imperialistic and they like to think that they invented all the best things. In this case that's manifestly not true.

David Hume, the great Scottish philosopher, reckoned that feeling was at the root of ethics – you see someone lying in the road in pain and you feel for them. I think that's probably right. Most of our solidarity with one another is because we are human too: I bleed, I can feel pain, I identify with you when you suffer the same adversities. Obviously, in order to work out policies and an ethical system, you also need to apply reason. Reason might say, 'in order to help you I'm going to have to inflict pain on you, because you've got a ruptured appendix and I need to operate'. Reason orders and marshals ways of doing good things, but I think you're prompted to do the good thing by a sense of fellow feeling. The Golden Rule probably sums it up. I like the negative form best: 'don't do to others what you wouldn't like done to you'. I'm not so sure of the positive – 'do unto others etc'… I'm not so sure I like being done unto.

I still think of myself as a Christian, but in an attenuated, humanistic way – I see Christianity as an art form rather than as a body of revealed absolute truth. I like many of its values once they've been separated from the packaging. The thing I'm more and more allergic to is people trying to evangelise other people into their particular take on things.

In his programme **The Root of all Evil**, the biologist Richard Dawkins quoted a thinker who said that bad people do bad things, and good people do good things, but only religion persuades good people to do bad things. It's a bit sweeping, but it's true. Think of the tortures during the Inquisition: it was better to make others suffer physical torture in this life, so that they would recant their heresies and on death be issued into eternal bliss – an example of people doing a bad thing for a good reason, as determined by a faith. However, I think that criticism can be levelled at all ideologies, whether religious or not. There's a dreadful warning there about the power big ideas can have over us.

for thoughts on…

→ 039
Anthony Grayling
on spirituality and design

→ 085
The Golden Rule

→ 137
Sheila Levrant de Bretteville
on inclusion

LR

You have written about 'opposing goods' as an alternative to thinking of good versus evil. Can you explain this idea and its connection with tolerance and understanding?

RH

I'm not saying that there aren't real psychopaths who lack moral sense and whom we might think of as ill. But broadly I agree with the philosopher Hegel, who said that most human conflict is fought between rival versions of the good and very rarely between an obvious good and an obvious evil. After all, who would side with an obvious evil? Even Nazi Germany probably began in most people's minds as an appropriate response to the political and social confusions of the time. One of the difficulties we face today is how to get into the shoes of people we radically disagree with and are therefore tempted to demonise. If we are not careful we can fall into the kind of dualism that divides the world into light and darkness, very much along the lines of George Bush's 'axis of evil'. I hate closed societies, but I also need to understand that they're often based on fear of the systems that are thought to be out to destroy values these closed systems hold dear.

I know you can take this too far, in that you can become so understanding that you become immobilised, but I hate the way liberals are now dismissed as floppy spineless people. The evolution of liberal democracy was based on profound ethical values. One basic principle is that tolerance is a fundamental and necessary value because human beings so notoriously disagree with one another. The Enlightenment in Europe was the result of the state's deep weariness with religious conflict. After those endless wars of religion, Voltaire and people like him said, '…enough already, you buggers are just going to have to learn to live with your disagreements, tolerate them, and stop killing people for them'. Tolerance wasn't a religious notion, it was secular.

It is a tough value, but it's not absolute, because it is impossible to tolerate absolutely everything, such as preaching hate, stirring up racial hatred, sexual hatred and so on – think of the things that we've recently outlawed in Europe. We don't tolerate people who say 'gays are faggots who ought to be thrown in jail'. We don't tolerate people who call black people niggers – and so on. Don't tell me liberalism is without a robust, sinewy moral code. But it also believes that on the whole we should leave people to get on with their own lives. John Stuart Mill's great essay **On Liberty** taught us that the state has the right to stop me harming you, it doesn't have the right to stop me harming myself.

Glossary of ethical thought

→ 068
Christian ethics

→ 073
Ethics of difference

LR

Graphic designers often feel conflicted,
as creative people who also offer a service.
Is there an ethical framework in which to
consider this?

RH

It strikes me that your profession is an
interdisciplinary one, not a pure one. It's a hybrid,
but there's nothing wrong with hybrids, in fact
most vigour in life is in these kind of cross-art art
forms. You're probably more like architects than
autonomous visual artists. In many ways this is one
of the most influential art forms. I think the grace
and beauty of public space can help to civilise
people, just as ugly public space can brutalise them.
Take an American diner – the old aluminium, shiny
cruiser type – there was a beauty in that and it was
absolutely functional. There is an ethic in design that
works well and is aesthetically enriching.

There is a current philosophical debate in the arts
community about the difference between an
instrumental and an intrinsic good. An instrumental
good is something that's good for something else,
whereas an intrinsic good is something that's good
in itself. The argument around fine art is that its
value lies in its being produced for its own sake not
for social regeneration or social renewal – but in
fact it's always been both, it's never been just one.
Good art is also good for other things. So good
design will please your client, it will maybe help
a product sell better, but it also improves life for
everyone because it can become something that's
lovely in its own right.

Take the new **Guardian** newspaper as an example.
It's beautiful. The people responsible have achieved
something there. The paper needed to change,
the day of the broadsheet was over, but the tabloid
is horrible so they borrowed the Berliner format
and certainly enhanced it. It's a joy to read. The
quality of the photography, everything, the layout,
the design – you've bought this paper at your
newsagent, it cost you 75p, but you're dealing with
a piece of quality. So you get all these virtuous
circles. This is the best of mass production because
it makes something of quality cheap and accessible.

for thoughts on...

LR
Designers often feel insecure and wary
that humility is an aspect of ethics
that compromises the quality of their
work. Is it possible to be self-effacing
and produce good work?

RH

There's nothing wrong with having a modest
ethic as a graphic designer. In a sense there's
a contract, a covenant between you and the people
you're working for – obviously you don't want to
cheat them, that's part of your ethic, you want to do
the best for them. Maybe what you also need is an
ethic of servant-hood, one based on the notion that
helping other people is a good thing to do. There
is a strong theological tradition that we are here to
facilitate the good life for one another. This is an
attitude that is basic to Christianity. God comes
among us not to lord it over us, but as a servant,
to amplify our life and make it more abundant.
That would be a wonderful ethic for any public
servant to have, so why not a designer?

I understand that there's a conflict, because artists
often want to be prophetic individuals, but I suspect
that a lot of what makes design valuable isn't that
it is unique or pioneering. If we look at journalism
again as an example, it is a skill that can become an
art. If you set out to provide a good service, to get
this truth over, to describe this event, to delight
someone with a short story, it can become an art,
something superior by virtue of the mystery of
grace. I would have thought that that's the right way
round – art coming almost by accident. So maybe
in addition to servant-hood you need a certain kind
of humility before art.

You refer to insecurity. Of course really big, secure
people are not posturing all the time, they do not
always have to assert their creativity. There are
some astonishingly gifted people. That's where envy
comes in, which is sorrow at another's good. It's not
even a kind of avarice, where you want what the
other person has – envy is when a person has a gift
and does something good and that makes you sad.
This makes it the meanest sin in the book. All the
other sins have a positive end, they're a good thing
gone slightly wrong – gluttony, lust, all that. But
envy has no positive outcome at all. It's not an
excess of wanting something, it's a deprivation, an
inability to rejoice in the gifts another person has,
and be grateful for them.

LR
Designers are generally tools of capitalism.
Are there approaches that designers
could take to make this role more ethical?

RH

The market is a glorious thing, but it is also
a monster that devours its children. Many of us,
designers included, have to admit to being
prostitutes in that sense – selling a talent on
behalf of this great monster, the most terrifyingly
powerful thing on the globe. Maybe the answer is
not to deal with it through your art, but to take an
interest in the politics and philosophy of the market.
Maybe it's as citizens you should be asking these
questions. Okay we serve this thing that is good
at delivering Reebok shoes and interesting coffee
and cheeses, but it is also capable of despoiling
the environment and flattening complete cultures,
so maybe we should be critically interested in
the thing we're serving.

There's nothing wrong with making money, and
there's nothing wrong with exploiting your talent,
but I think you probably need a philosophy that
says in addition to that: I'm a citizen of the world;
I want the world to be as good a place for me and
my children and my grandchildren as it can be;
so I can't simply be the hand that draws or the eye
behind the lens; I also need to be committed
and engaged in other areas. One way to make
a difference is through voluntary work for example.
That's one way of putting something back and
Okay if it's guilt that's making you do it, who cares?
Maybe doing design work for NGOs and so on is
another way – it's clearly balancing the imbalance
between good and evil in the world. What I think
is always reprehensible is for people not to
be honest about the reality of what they're doing.

I was on the Human Fertilisation and Embryology
Authority and was surprised by the collusion
between the gynaecology and fertility business
and drug companies. Doctors do great work,
drug companies do great work, but everything
is corruptible, so what you need then is to be
politicised and to challenge the use to which the
good thing is being put, rather than thinking
that somehow your art, mystically of its own power,
will somehow cleanse the thing – it won't.

for thoughts on...

LR

The market relies on constant demand, and design is used to increase this. Surely this means that design, as we know it, will become unsustainable?

RH

The whole nature of the market is to increase discontent. There's something deeply flawed about it. On the other hand people say it's that discontent that has made us the most creative animals on the planet. As well as despoiling the planet we painted the Sistine Chapel, we built St Peter's in Rome and St Paul's in London, and York Minster – it's all part of the same package in a way.

We now need to scare ourselves about the dark side of our discontent and respond to it. I like something the Italian political theorist Antonio Gramsci said: that we should be pessimists of the intellect and optimists of the will. The idea being that yes, a lot of bad things happen; people are aggressive and greedy and avaricious; but they're also capable of astonishing kindness and rationality. We're aware now that we're polluting the planet, so we're trying, however belatedly, to do something about it. Big companies can be enlightened too, when they recognise that they belong to the planet as well.

Then I have to admit that there's so much about the modern world that I do like and love – the variety of cuisines, the comfortable houses. When the philosopher AC Grayling is asked if he believes in progress, whether things are getting better, he always cites the example of dentistry. We don't now have to live with permanent mouth pain the way our ancestors did, who spent a lot of time in sheer agony. Okay you could get a tooth pulled, but can you imagine the pain of waiting while your teeth just died on you? So, some things are better and some things are worse – there's always loss and gain. I also think central heating's pretty good!

Glossary of ethical thought

→ 066
Buddhism

Delyth Morgan studied science
at London University where she was
student union president, before entering
the voluntary sector as a campaigner,
first at Shelter and later on childcare issues
and as a patient advocate. She was the first
Chief Executive of Breakthrough Breast
Cancer, where she orchestrated high-profile
campaigns and significantly increased public
awareness of the disease. A member of
the NHS Modernisation Board and the NHS
National Cancer Taskforce, she has also
chaired the Patient Choice Task Group on
Primary Care. Having joined the Labour Party
at 18, she was introduced to the House
of Lords in 2004 as Baroness Morgan of
Drefelin – the youngest woman peer. Her
current appointments include Secretary
of the All-Party Group for the Voluntary and
Community Sector and Vice Chair of the
All-Party Parliamentary Group on Cancer.
[British, born 1961]

LR

Having political power makes it possible
to make a societal difference – hopefully for
the good. To be a successful political figure
requires fervour and passion, tempered by
objectivity and respect for the opposition's
view. The ethical dilemmas in trying to be fair
are multifarious and inexhaustible. Now a
member of the House of Lords, Delyth Morgan
has been involved indirectly and directly
in politics all her adult life. She believes
it is possible to change things for the better
and, having worked in communications,
is also aware that graphic design can play
an important role in this process.

LR
Design is highly competitive. Designers often feel insecure, which engenders bad behaviour. Aren't notions of collective responsibility at odds with an economy like ours, in which people succeed or fail by their own endeavours?

DM

I used to find that really hard. When I was a teenager I used to think that everyone should be paid the same as a reflection of our equal value. But as I got older I realised that some people do really try a lot harder than others and that therefore maybe they should be allowed to have a greater share of the fruits of their work. There are questions about exploitation though. Say someone develops a very successful product. You know, a designer comes up with an ingenious design. Good for them – but then someone has to put it together and make it. Is it right if these people are poorly paid relative to the entrepreneurial designer? They are mutually dependent, after all.

I believe that we are better served by being part of a community and helping each other, than as individuals fighting for our own turf. I was motivated by the idea of us holding hands together and trying to create a better world together. As you know, I used to commission graphic design and so obviously I'm aware of how insecure the self-employed designer feels. I think it is a very wise person who understands how unimportant they are in the grand scheme of things and can rise above their immediate feelings of vulnerability and fragility. The important thing is to ask 'What am I really trying to do?', 'What are my measures of success?'. For a designer there are perhaps sometimes incompatible desires, like wanting to make a difference in the world and be rated from a pure design perspective among your peers. I understand that without feelings of self-worth it is hard to carry on, and so understandably we seek approval from many sources.

I feel accountable to a matrix of people and would hope to have approval from them all. Because of my background this would range from the voluntary sector to the Labour Party, who after all put me in the House of Lords. Then there's my local party, myself, and my family and friends. They are very important to me – their disapproval would be very hard.

for thoughts on...

→ 127
Simon Esterson
on behaviour

→ 177
Ken Garland
on political engagement

→ 185
Pat Kahn
on making a difference

LR

Designers can fall prey to dogma. Even if politicians start off wanting to do good, doesn't the mixture of ideology and power get the better of them?

DM

People get involved in politics for lots of reasons. I was initially influenced by my parents, who came from South Wales and were active in the Labour Party because it was the party of the working class. I became politically active in the early '80s – that was when my loyalties and perspective were formed. I was motivated by the idea of collective action. It was clear to me that you can only make a difference if you're prepared to get involved and take responsibility.

This obviously requires taking power. However, in order to win elections there are inevitable trade-offs between ideals and what is practically possible. The risks are that either you are tied too heavily to theory, and lose a sense of what you're actually doing, or that you become dislocated from the ideology and lose sight of your objectives. If you have a real conviction then there should be a point of compromise beyond which you won't go, because of the implications for everything else that you believe. That's the difficult bit – particularly for the Left, I think.

Then there is the issue of personal convictions and party loyalties. The collective voice is very important. If you stand for election as a representative of a political party and then want to change the party line, the debate about change should be within the party. If your problems can't be reconciled you should leave. If you're holding office, how can you be publicly very critical? What are you doing representing the party if you don't believe in what the party's doing?

I try to remind myself of the seven principles of public life: selflessness, integrity, objectivity, accountability, openness, honesty and leadership. For me it's not about whether I like power, it's whether the ideas of the party work, whether it really delivers what it says on the tin: to make people more equal and to make society fairer and better. Contrary to popular belief, I do think that most people in politics are motivated to do good. For example, whether I agree with him or not, if I thought Tony Blair was only acting out of self-interest rather than conviction that would make my role untenable. What motivates people matters considerably, it affects your trust, so to this extent intention is as important as outcome.

Glossary of ethical thought

→ 068
Stoicism

→ 073
Ethics of difference

LR
Graphic design is about communicating messages. It can also visually enrich people's lives. For me this makes it a political activity. What issues do you think this raises for designers?

DM
Firstly, I think it's going to be quite hard to make an impact if your aim is to improve people's quality of life by producing aesthetically pleasing graphics alone. But if you're trying to convince people to do something or to understand something by producing strong design then I can see you'd make an impact. For me making a difference rates really highly.

So, if you see your purpose as communicating a message, then you've got to have something to say. This inevitably means you have a perspective, which does make it a political activity. I guess the issues therefore revolve around context. Who you're working for, who you're trying to communicate with, and how you choose to do that, what kind of tools you use – even the kind of paper you use is a statement and that's before you even put anything on it.

I can see that choice of client is important, although perhaps this raises issues of professionalism versus artistry. It would be hard for a designer to approach this as objectively as a barrister, for example. Theirs is an intellectual exercise as they interpret the letter of the law. There are moments of inspiration, I'm sure, but ultimately it's down to whether the law works. But if a designer is working with a client without empathy for the issue, then I imagine that could impede their ability to communicate effectively and creatively. I'm sure you can go through the motions, but it may not actually work as well.

That said, if a designer can't disengage emotionally that could limit their ability to solve a design problem. When I was Chief Executive at Breakthrough Breast Cancer, for example, I found that by grabbing people's attention emotionally, a debate was fuelled and breast cancer moved up the agenda. However, this mustn't cloud the debate. To make effective decisions you have to apply reason.

for thoughts on...

→ 026–031, 088–093
Designer responsibility

→ 117
Michael Marriott on politics and design

→ 134
Chris de Bode on politics and photojournalism

LR
How do you manage to defend the rights
of the individual or minority against
the idea of the greatest happiness for the
greatest number of people?

DM

That's the constant tension in politics. An example
would be Herceptin. Here is a breast cancer drug
that could save an individual's life – could, not
definitely – and it's very expensive. So do you put
NHS resources into buying a very expensive drug
for a few, when in so doing you're denying many
the resources that could help them? The only
way you can deal with these kinds of decisions is
through democracy – debate and discussion.
There's no right answer.

It was much more clear-cut when I was at
Breakthrough. I just wanted to raise lots of money
to spend on excellent research, in the hope that
something interesting would come out of it
to help save lives and create some kind of new
understanding in the long run.

My focus now that I am in the House of Lords is
different. I want to encourage debate about greater
equality and equity. A current debate is whether
it matters if the gap between rich and poor gets
bigger. One argument is that as long as the poor are
getting richer, the disparity doesn't matter. But for
me it's not just about wealth, it's about fairness.

Lord Layard, an LSE Emeritus Professor who is also
in the Lords, has written a book about happiness
that is really quite amazing given he is a serious
economist. His argument is that we're going to
continue to get better off as a society, but that it is
relative wealth that affects somebody's happiness
much more than what they acquire. If everyone
else has a television it is undermining not to have
one – but if nobody has one it's not.

Of course politics requires objectivity. I used to
assume that everyone would want what I wanted,
but I had contact with the world of research
both at Breakthrough and the National Asthma
Campaign, and became aware of the value of
evidence and consultation. Your argument shouldn't
be determined by personal beliefs alone, but set
in a wider context. So, if I believe all children should
have a particular kind of education I see the value
in asking what do children, parents and teachers
think. Not everybody wants the same thing, but
I want everyone to have the same opportunities.

Glossary of ethical thought

→ 069
Utilitarianism

→ 071
Kierkegaard
Nietzsche

Anthony Grayling suggested that it is possible to arrive at an ethical code of practice for graphic design by considering 'a way of being' that draws on examples of responsible or well-intentioned practice. Various themes recurred in these theoretical interviews that might help us do just that:

Being responsible

With greater freedom has come greater responsibility. As Anthony Grayling said, 'designers find themselves in a spider's web of duties'; responsible to clients, end-users, colleagues, themselves and their work, as well as the wider world and society at large. How might a designer evaluate the conflicting interests of those to whom they are responsible?

Professionalism

There are moral obligations as a professional. Jacqueline Roach explained the overarching professional principles that govern in the law. What are the general and specific professional principles that can be applied in design?

Freedom and ideology

Freedom of speech and freedom of choice are, within reason, basic human rights. Is it then our role to censor by refusing certain sorts of work? Delyth Morgan talked of the need to strike a balance between ideals and realities. How might designers stay true to their core beliefs and concerns while being tolerant and open to the views of others?

Equality and reciprocity

Considering all people as equal, regardless of difference, is a basic human right. Richard Holloway referred to the Golden Rule, common to most religious and secular belief structures: 'don't do to others what you wouldn't like done to you'. How might these notions shape design practice?

The market economy

The free market has delivered enormous choice, but design is playing a part in encouraging insatiable desire with the resultant discontent and environmental consequences. Capitalism thrives by encouraging the individual and the entrepreneur – which is perfect for many designers. But Delyth Morgan argued that 'we are better served by being part of a community and helping each other'. Jacqueline Roach described most of us as 'worker bees'; Richard Holloway argued for a modest ethic of design. But design is a competitive business that requires enormous self-belief and self-determination. How might we succeed as designers without behaving badly?

Opposing versions of good

Richard Holloway said that ethical divisions are often not drawn between the good and the bad, but between opposing versions of good. He talked of intrinsic and instrumental 'goods' within the arts. How might we arrive at a more useful and accurate way to assess the value of design work?

Happiness and quality of life

Design can make others happy, as well as the designer who created it. Is design that makes the majority happy more valuable than that which appeals to the few? Anthony Grayling said 'every aspect of our lives is touched constantly by considerations of the quality of our experience. So there is a deep connection between the aesthetic and the ethical for this reason'. How might a designer try to improve the quality of life for others?

Naomi Goulder studied philosophy at Cambridge University and Harvard. She met Ronnie Cooke Newhouse while working briefly at **i-D** magazine, and joined her studio where she worked for many years on jobs including advertising campaigns for the fashion house Comme des Garçons. Goulder's guiding preoccupation is with the particularity of the individual and she is currently writing her PhD at Birkbeck College, University of London on the subject of freedom, rationality and the metaphysics of (individual) self. She is the editor of the **Encyclopedia of British Philosophy** with AC Grayling and Andrew Pyle, and writes each day in the British Library. [British, born 1976]

Frederik Willemarck studied economics at the University of Ghent and economics and philosophy at University College London. He is currently a PhD student in philosophy at Birkbeck College, University of London. His thesis is concerned with theories of spontaneous social order, and investigates the implications of these theories in relation to the idea of political freedom. Willemarck is also a writer of short stories and book reviews, some of which have appeared in the weekly literary supplement of the Belgian newspaper **De Standaard**. [Belgian, born 1976]

This isn't a philosophy book but ethics, or moral philosophy, is its starting point. The history of ethics is the history of mankind, and so what follows is inevitably a selective introduction. In chronological order, it covers those ethical movements that have been most influential on western thought, as well as major influences from the East. Simplifications have been made in pursuit of clarity, but key figures and texts have been cited so that the interested reader can inquire further. Considering design practice against these ideas helps in assessing design contributions, however small, relative to the wider world.

Buddhism

Buddhism comprises many schools of thought that all go back to the teachings of the Indian Prince Siddhartha Gautama (sixth–fifth century BC), who was eventually called Buddha. 'Buddha' means 'the awakened one', and Buddha reached this state of insight after years of travel, study and meditation. Having become awakened, he started preaching the wisdom he had acquired. An important aspect of his teachings is the idea of selflessness, in both metaphysical and ethical senses.

Persons and things, according to Buddhism, have no essences and cannot be sustained over time. Unfortunately, people have a natural yearning for identity and stability that is impossible to satisfy. This leads to frustration, with the general consequence that life is painful and full of suffering. Individuals are locked into a life of suffering by a continuous process of becoming and rebirth, from which there is no escape as long as one remains ignorant and does not awaken.

'Nirvana' is the state in which a person is liberated from this permanent cycle of pain and suffering. It involves an insight into the lack of essence of things and persons, and is characterised by a sense of calmness and a complete lack of desires. The optimistic part of Buddha's teachings is that every person can reach nirvana. Buddhism describes how it can be reached, and this, in fact, constitutes the ethical part of this system of thought.

Buddhist ethics cover many aspects of personal life and have consequences for how individuals should act, speak and live. In addition, Buddhism gives advice concerning intellectual activities and meditation. The underlying ideals of Buddhist ethical teachings are clarity, a lack of desires and compassion. It is believed that a person who follows these teachings will acquire insight and eventually reach nirvana.

Confucianism

Confucius was a chinese philosopher who lived in the sixth–fifth century BC. 'Confucius' is the latinised name for 'K'ung fu-tzu' or 'Kong the master'. Confucius was a member of a social group called 'Ju' that engaged in collective rituals. Apart from this background in ritual practices, Confucius was concerned with the social and political situation of his time. His teachings have a political dimension, and are pervaded by the belief that personal perfection – mainly through a restoration of traditional values – can lead to an improvement of the general political situation. Although Confucius's original teachings gave rise to different schools of thought, the concern with the social and the political still plays a central role in contemporary Confucian philosophy.

Confucianism, like many ancient philosophies, describes an ideal way of life, and teaches how the virtuous or wise man should live. A central element of Confucian ethics is that one should have a basic concern for all living beings. With regard to people, Confucianism prescribes that one should approach others with respect and also in a way that conforms to a general idea of what is right. It is important to note that there are no rules to determine the right action. Instead, what is right can only be decided by taking into account the circumstances in which one finds oneself.

Confucianism advocates gradual development towards an ideal way of life. Underlying its teachings is the belief that exemplary behaviour of rulers and teachers will eventually induce people to change their own conduct. These changes in personal conduct, in turn, will lead to an improvement of the general political situation.

Platonism

Plato (c429–347 BC) held that the world is divided into reality and appearance. Appearance is the obvious and everyday world that we experience through our senses. Reality is a realm of eternal and perfect 'forms' that can only be discerned through the rational intellect, and which are the only proper objects of knowledge. A way to think of these 'forms' is as templates, in rather the way that a mathematician's ideal triangle is a template for the actual triangle drawn on paper. The greatest form of all, for Plato, was the form of the 'good'.

There is optimism in the Platonic thesis that the real world is all good, if only we can live up to it. Plato's vision of reality as inherently good and beautiful led him to claim that evil is just a kind of failure to achieve full realisation. A virtuous person manifests a real soul, whereas an evil person manifests mere physical 'appearance'. Plato's conviction that the good for one person is harmonious with the good for all, along with his special confidence in the powers of pure reason, eventually led him to propose an ideal 'republic' ruled by philosophers. This political vision was compared by later thinkers to modern totalitarian regimes, highlighting problematic aspects of his wider theory. Nonetheless, Platonic confidence in goodness, reason and metaphysical harmony has been profoundly influential.

Aristotelianism

Though rejecting Plato's metaphysics of transcendental 'forms', Aristotle (384–322 BC) shared his teacher's confidence in the idea of a highest good for man. 'Eudaimonia', often translated as 'happiness', but better captured as 'living well' or 'flourishing', is (he thought) the natural function and ultimate purpose of human action. Aristotle's ethical writings attempt to spell out in more detail this best life for a human being, which turns out to include the exercise of virtues such as justice, courage and generosity. Just as the function of a knife is to cut, so a good knife is one that cuts well; Aristotle claimed that the function of man is to be virtuous, so the excellent life is one of virtue.

Unlike later Christian ideas of morality, which often set doing one's duty against being happy, for Aristotle human excellence coincides with happiness. The virtues are conceived as inextricably linked with such goods as friendship, wealth and beauty. (To put it crudely, an Aristotelian might think that a person could not be generous if he was penniless and ugly – any attempts he might make at generosity would be more ridiculous than noble.)

Unlike Plato, Aristotle did not think that ethical goodness could be learned through mere rational reflection, or codified in any set of ethical rules. Instead, ethical character is acquired naturally through growing up in human culture.

In 306 BC, Epicurus (c341–270 BC) founded a community just outside Athens called 'The Garden'. His teachings there combined the idea that the world consists of atoms, with an ethical outlook aimed at worldly happiness.

The good life, according to Epicurus, takes place far away from public affairs and is lived in small communities of like-minded people and friends. It is characterised by a lack of physical pain and a peaceful state of mind. Although Epicurus was 'hedonistic' in claiming that the ultimate good is pleasure, it is generally accepted that he was not an advocate of excess, but rather of a life that was moderated and even austere.

Unlike Epicureanism, stoicism is not based on the writings of one author but was developed over centuries by a variety of thinkers. It was founded by Zeno of Citium (334–262 BC), and played a very influential role in Roman thought.

Stoicism advocates a conception of the good life in which reason prevails. The virtuous man should be guided by reason and avoid strong emotions, such as fear and distress. He understands that he has no complete control of the outcome of his actions, and therefore he will not be in distress when an action fails to bring about an intended outcome. A person's eventual accomplishments are less important than his intentions and motivations.

Stoicism teaches that the virtuous man should take up responsibilities and actively partake in public life, rather than living only among friends and like-minded people as advocated by Epicurus.

The most important early Christian philosophical thinker is St Augustine (354–430), who was born and lived in northern Africa. Augustine had a conversion experience in 386 in the garden where he lived, and went on to write numerous works, including **Confessions** and **The City of God**, which set an authoritative framework for subsequent Christian ethics. Augustine notably emphasised the moral significance of motives over actions. He thought the ultimate motive that gave value to all the others was love of God.

Augustine saw human life as a punishment for Adam's original sin, and thought we could achieve redemption only through overcoming our natural inclinations towards sinfulness by orientating ourselves towards God. The medieval Christian philosopher, St Thomas of Aquinas (c1225–74), developed the Augustinian view in a more optimistic direction, denying that human nature is naturally sinful, and claiming instead that our faculty of reason quite naturally leads us towards morality. He believed that God, being benevolent, gave us reason so that we would be naturally orientated in the right direction.

The Christian focus on inner conscience as opposed to outward action, and on the central Christian virtues of faith, hope and love, comes to striking – and rather different – modern expressions in the work of Kant and Kierkegaard.

Utilitarianism

Utilitarianism is a theory about what is right. In its most well-known form, it provides an answer to the question 'What is the right thing to do?', or 'Which action is the right one to take?'. Utilitarianism evaluates actions according to their consequences, and measures these consequences according to some welfare or 'utility' measurement. As a general rule, the right action to take is the action that maximises welfare.

There are different ways in which the rather abstract notion of welfare can be filled out. Traditional utilitarians were hedonists, arguing that the right action is that which brings about the greatest pleasure or happiness. Utilitarianism does not distinguish between the pleasure of different persons: not only is the pleasure of the person who undertakes the action taken into account, but also the pleasure of other people involved. For example, imagine a couple where the wife wants to go on holiday on her own. If the pain suffered by the husband because of loneliness offsets the wife's pleasure gained by travelling alone, a utilitarian would advise the wife to stay with her husband, and not go travelling.

Utilitarianism in its modern form has as its two main proponents Jeremy Bentham (1748–1832), who gave the theory its first systematic treatment, and John Stuart Mill (1806–73). Although the theory has been criticised on many fronts, among other things for its disregard of people over abstract notions such as pleasure, its influence remains significant in contemporary philosophy and in the social sciences.

Kantian ethics

Immanuel Kant (1724–1804) identified a single path towards human freedom, rationality and morality. He claimed that a person could achieve all three by following a principle called the 'Categorical Imperative'. This principle tells a person to act only on motives that he could at the same time 'will' (intend) as universal laws. According to Kant, any motive that fails this test is one that a person has a moral duty not to act upon. The motive 'I will lie', for example, fails the test: if everyone was a deceiver then no one would ever believe anyone, and lying would be impossible. Accordingly, we have a strict duty not to lie.

Kant's Categorical Imperative in its most famous formulation generates duties that many have thought to be insane (could a person really have a duty not to lie to a murderer about where a child is?). But alternative formulations of the principle are often found attractive – especially Kant's idea that we should never treat humanity merely as a means, but always as an end in itself. Kant's conviction that the dictates of morality, rationality and freedom must coincide was of major significance to the development of German idealism. His emphasis on individual freedom may also be traced through the development of romanticism and existentialism.

Idealism

Idealist philosophers take the most basic feature of reality to be the mind, or the 'rational' principles by which the mind operates. The most important idealism after Kant is in the German tradition of Johann Gottlieb Fichte (1762–1814), GWF Hegel (1770–1831) and Arthur Schopenhauer (1788–1860). These thinkers followed Kant in emphasising rational thought and freedom over sensation and subjection to scientific law, but developed his ideas with an explicitly social and historical emphasis. They conceived the realm of rational thought as essentially tied to the social world, and as evolving through the progress of human civilisation. If human beings are essentially rational, and rationality is essentially social, then (they argued) human beings are themselves essentially social. Self-interest is therefore subsumed into a more broadly social or ethical conception of flourishing. Individual freedom and self-realisation are to be achieved through identification with, and submission to, the rational 'world spirit' (or universal will).

Both Hegel and Fichte increasingly wrote as if the authority of the universal will was manifest specifically in the German state, and both have been accused of nationalism. Schopenhauer's view developed rather differently. Though claiming that the individual will should be subsumed by the universal will, he thought that even the universal will should ultimately be transcended. Influenced by Buddhist and Stoic ethics, Schopenhauer claimed that all will (or desire) is a source of illusion and suffering, and he promoted an ethics of ascetic renunciation.

The influences of German idealism are various. The place given to man within an intelligibly structured nature was important for the development of romanticism, and was connected with various artistic and literary figures, most famously Goethe. The idea of an inexorably evolving social order was important also to Marxism (in fact, Marx wrote some of his first works on Hegel). Many influential Anglo-American figures of the late nineteenth and early twentieth century built upon the work of the German idealists (notably TH Green, FH Bradley and Josiah Royce). The conception of man as an essentially social being is also reprised in recent 'communitarian' political thought.

Marxism

Karl Marx (1818–83) is perhaps the most important social theorist of modern times. Although he was born in the German city of Trier, he spent most of his working life in London.

An influential idea developed in Marx's early writings – most famously in the so-called **Paris Manuscripts** of 1844 – is the concept of alienation. The notion stems from the work of the philosopher GWF Hegel, but Marx gave it a new interpretation by revealing its economic and social origins.

According to Marx, people find themselves in a state of alienation when they are unable to use their essential human capacities. In an ideal situation, people would fulfil their capacities and fully realise themselves. They would thereby become actual (rather than merely potential) things in the world, and would accordingly be able to see themselves as adequately expressed in it.

The predicament of modern man living in an industrialised age is that he is condemned to meaningless labour. He is not able to relate himself to his labour, nor does he recognise himself in the products that are the result of this labour. In this sense, it can be said that the (proletarian) labourer is alienated from his products, and from himself.

For Marx, the ideal of a human being who overcomes alienation and uses his capacities to attain a state of self-realisation is exemplified in the person of the artist. The work of an artist is pure creativity, and goes beyond the satisfaction of mere life-sustaining needs for food, clothing and shelter. Instead, the artist gives expression to his life and being.

Kierkegaard and Nietzsche

Transcendentalism

Søren Kierkegaard (1813–55) and Friedrich Nietzsche (1844–1900) are often grouped together as precursors to existentialism. Though their metaphysical systems differ widely – Kierkegaard exulted the 'religious', whereas Nietzsche wrote of the 'death of God' – there is some point to this association. An extreme, often idiosyncratic, individualism unites Kierkegaard and Nietzsche, along with a preoccupation with the possibilities for individual authenticity and the forces that cripple it.

Perhaps unsurprisingly given that ethics traditionally accords value to the collective over the individual, the individualistic impulse is developed by both thinkers as a kind of anti-ethic, or as an attempt to go beyond ethics (which is not the same as nihilism, or the complete denial of value). Kierkegaard diagnosed three stages of human development, of which the ethical is only the second: highest of all is the 'religious', where one is moved not by impulses towards pleasure, nor by moral rules, but rather by personal conviction, or faith. Nietzsche held up as ideal those rare individuals who are strong enough to create values of their own, and is famous for criticising Christian morality as merely a construction by the weak to protect them from the strong.

In a world in which the only values are individual values, both Kierkegaard and Nietzsche thus suggested that it is necessary to overcome the external forces of social morality and to act 'authentically' on values to which you are absolutely committed. These values are part of your nature, and to act on them is to be free.

Transcendentalism is associated with a loose coalition of thinkers centred around New England in the mid-nineteenth century. Led by Ralph Waldo Emerson (1803–82), these thinkers devised a modified European romanticism in response to what they considered to be America's destructive path of industrialisation, commercialism and philistinism. The transcendentalists attempted to reformulate the ideals of the American Revolution through appeal to nature and the 'simple life'. Theirs was accordingly a hybrid movement, which harnessed the non-rational values of wilderness, nature and primitivism to the absolute, moral conviction of the Puritans. The transcendentalists advocated an ascetic life, through which moral renewal would result from instinctual reform at the individual level, creating what Emerson described as a 'purity of conscience'.

The exemplary text of transcendentalism is Henry David Thoreau's **Walden** (1854), in which the writer describes his retreat to a solitary life in the woods, spent observing, celebrating and subsisting in his natural surroundings. Through its affirmation of wilderness as an improving tool for mankind, transcendentalism has created a lasting legacy in American culture, which combines powerfully with the revolutionary ideals of freedom and individualism. However, the ultimate failure of the alternative communities and lifestyles spawned by followers of Emerson (such as Thoreau's at Walden Pond and the utopian 'Fruitlands' farm) suggests that the transcendental fantasy of a prelapsarian life in nature may, ultimately, be of more symbolic than practical value.

Emotivism

Two philosophical tendencies were prevalent in Western philosophy in the early years of the twentieth century. The first was a rejection of the idea that moral values exist in the world. The second was an impulse to conduct philosophy by means of the analysis of language. These tendencies coalesced briefly in the development of emotivism. Although various theories fall under the 'emotivist' heading, its central idea is that moral utterances serve primarily to express the speaker's emotions or emotional attitudes, or to prompt such emotions or attitudes to arise in others. Moral judgements do not aim to state facts, but rather to express or elicit feelings. Emotivism is sometimes referred to as the 'boo/hurrah' theory, because it takes moral judgements to be little more than outbursts of that kind. CL Stevenson (1908–79), AJ Ayer (1910–89) and – with a distinctive version – RM Hare (1919–2002) are the best-known proponents of emotivist theories.

Though most would agree that moral judgements have expressive and emotional functions, the thesis that this gives the primary sense of moral judgements soon came to seem implausible. One of the most obvious problems with the view is that it cannot account for meaningful moral disagreement. If, as emotivists suppose, no one ever really aims to state moral facts and all that is at stake in moral argument is people's emotions, then it looks like ethics does not have the importance that we intuitively take it to have. Since the 1960s, few philosophers have endorsed emotivism.

Existentialism

Existentialism emerged as a distinctive philosophical movement in the first half of the twentieth century, notably in the work of Edmund Husserl (1859–1938), Martin Heidegger (1889–1976), Jean-Paul Sartre (1905–80) and Albert Camus (1913–60), though many of its ideas can be found in the earlier writings of Dostoevsky, Kierkegaard and Nietzsche.

The basic existentialist insight is that there is no objective 'human nature' against which individuals can be measured or judged. Human existence has no predetermined meaning or purpose, and it is up to each individual to create himself and the values by which he lives. Existentialists thus make a fundamental distinction between the human individual (which exists 'for-itself' and is essentially free), and mere objects (which exist only 'in-themselves', and are subject to deterministic laws of nature). And the freedom essential to the human condition is conceived by existentialists both as a liberation and as a responsibility – because we are free, the choices that we make are fraught with anxiety ('nausea' or 'anguish'). Writers such as Husserl and Heidegger developed a 'phenomenological' method that focused on individual acts of consciousness, which were taken to be integral to freedom.

Though existentialism often conflicts with traditional moralities, it brings with it its own individualistic ideal of freedom and authenticity. Many of the existentialists were actively engaged in politics (though not always helpfully to the cause of the freedom they so prized). Despite the fact that his criticisms of communism (in **The Rebel**) led to his falling out with Sartre, Camus probably makes the most compelling existentialist arguments for political freedom.

Virtue ethics

Ethics of difference

Virtue ethics accord basic ethical value to character traits, as opposed, for example, to actions or motives. The original virtue ethicists are the ancient Greeks, but opponents of Kantian and utilitarian ethics through the centuries have often focused on virtues of character. Notable in this later virtue tradition are the eighteenth century 'moral sense' theorists, especially David Hume (1711–76), along with certain prominent contemporary figures.

Since character traits are formed and given value within a society, rather than innately given or determined by God, virtue theorists tend to emphasise the ethical significance of tradition. Wittgenstein's claim in Philosophical Investigations (published posthumously, 1953) that the most basic features of our shared 'form of life' constitute a 'bedrock' that cannot meaningfully be questioned accordingly led to renewed interest in the virtues. Philippa Foot's **Virtues and Vices** (1978) and Alasdair MacIntyre's **After Virtue** (1981) are central texts in this revival.

It should be noted, however, that for Wittgenstein himself, reflections on our shared form of life undermine the very project of formulating an ethical theory – and lead rather into ethical mysticism.

Different cultures enshrine widely divergent ethical codes, and it is tempting to think that no single one of them has absolute authority. Faced with the great diversity of religious and cultural practices across the world, pursuit of a single answer to moral questions can seem inappropriate.

Relativists give up the search for absolute moral answers, and claim that moral questions can be asked (or answered) only relative to a context. An extreme relativist might say, for example, that terrorism is wrong for us (in our context), but right for terrorists (in theirs). But no serious thinker subscribes to extreme relativism, especially since it involves making a quite artificial distinction between 'our' context and 'theirs'. Ethics is more commonly viewed as relative to something general, like the human condition – and since this is not 'relative' in an especially interesting sense, few would accept the relativist label.

What might be called an 'ethics of difference' eschews relativist rhetoric while nonetheless taking seriously the insight that we need to respect difference, and examining its deeper philosophical consequences. It seeks to articulate forms of human understanding and interaction that accommodate differences, rather than disguising or undermining them. In this endeavour, it attempts to explode traditional (eg class-, gender-, race- or sexuality-based) assumptions embedded in our inherited language, institutions, and practices. But even though it rejects authoritarian values of the past, it does not give up hope of finding values that can be accepted by all.

Unsurprisingly, the ethics of difference tend to focus on traditionally oppressed or 'minority' groups. Thus 'feminist' philosophers are prominent in emphasising, for example, the moral significance of virtues such as 'caring' that have traditionally been overlooked in favour of more (supposedly) masculine virtues such as 'courage'. But the aim of the ethics of difference characteristically is to redress an existing imbalance between groups, rather than to privilege any single group above another.

Human Rights Act, 1998

An Act to give further effect to rights and freedoms guaranteed under the European Convention on Human Rights; to make provision with respect to holders of certain judicial offices who become judges of the European Court of Human Rights; and for connected purposes.
9 November 1998

The Convention Rights

1(1)
In this Act 'the Convention Rights' means the rights and fundamental freedoms set out in:

a
Articles 2 to 12 and 14 of the Convention,

b
Articles 1 to 3 of the First Protocol, and

c
Articles 1 and 2 of the Sixth Protocol, as read with Articles 16 to 18 of the Convention.

In 1998 the European Convention on Human Rights was incorporated into British law. Printed here are the Convention Rights, or the rights and fundamental freedoms set out in the Convention. This text enshrines the ethical values that underpin many societies. It is organised around basic principles that are useful to us in considering all ethical codes of practice.

Article 2
Right to life

1

Everyone's right to life shall be protected by law. No one shall be deprived of his life intentionally save in the execution of a sentence of a court following his conviction of a crime for which this penalty is provided by law.

2

Deprivation of life shall not be regarded as inflicted in contravention of this Article when it results from the use of force which is no more than absolutely necessary:

a

in defence of any person from unlawful violence;

b

in order to effect a lawful arrest or to prevent the escape of a person lawfully detained;

c

in action lawfully taken for the purpose of quelling a riot or insurrection.

Article 3
Prohibition of torture

No one shall be subjected to torture or to inhuman or degrading treatment or punishment.

Article 4
Prohibition of slavery and forced labour

1

No one shall be held in slavery or servitude.

2

No one shall be required to perform forced or compulsory labour.

3

For the purpose of this Article the term 'forced or compulsory labour' shall not include:

a

any work required to be done in the ordinary course of detention imposed according to the provisions of Article 5 of this Convention or during conditional release from such detention;

b

any service of a military character or, in case of conscientious objectors in countries where they are recognised, service exacted instead of compulsory military service;

c

any service exacted in case of an emergency or calamity threatening the life or well-being of the community;

d

any work or service which forms part of normal civic obligations.

Article 5
Right to liberty and security

1

Everyone has the right to liberty and security of person. No one shall be deprived of his liberty save in the following cases and in accordance with a procedure prescribed by law:

a

the lawful detention of a person after conviction by a competent court;

b

the lawful arrest or detention of a person for non-compliance with the lawful order of a court or in order to secure the fulfilment of any obligation prescribed by law;

c

the lawful arrest or detention of a person effected for the purpose of bringing him before the competent legal authority on reasonable suspicion of having committed an offence or when it is reasonably considered necessary to prevent his committing an offence or fleeing after having done so;

d

the detention of a minor by lawful order for the purpose of educational supervision or his lawful detention for the purpose of bringing him before the competent legal authority;

e

the lawful detention of persons for the prevention of the spreading of infectious diseases, of persons of unsound mind, alcoholics or drug addicts or vagrants;

f

the lawful arrest or detention of a person to prevent his effecting an unauthorised entry into the country or of a person against whom action is being taken with a view to deportation or extradition.

2

Everyone who is arrested shall be informed promptly, in a language which he understands, of the reasons for his arrest and of any charge against him.

3

Everyone arrested or detained in accordance with the provisions of paragraph 1(c) of this Article shall be brought promptly before a judge or other officer authorised by law to exercise judicial power and shall be entitled to trial within a reasonable time or to release pending trial. Release may be conditioned by guarantees to appear for trial.

4

Everyone who is deprived of his liberty by arrest or detention shall be entitled to take proceedings by which the lawfulness of his detention shall be decided speedily by a court and his release ordered if the detention is not lawful.

5

Everyone who has been the victim of arrest or detention in contravention of the provisions of this Article shall have an enforceable right to compensation.

Article 6
Right to a fair trial

1

In the determination of his civil rights and obligations or of any criminal charge against him, everyone is entitled to a fair and public hearing within a reasonable time by an independent and impartial tribunal established by law. Judgment shall be pronounced publicly but the press and public may be excluded from all or part of the trial in the interest of morals, public order or national security in a democratic society, where the interests of juveniles or the protection of the private life of the parties so require, or to the extent strictly necessary in the opinion of the court in special circumstances where publicity would prejudice the interests of justice.

2

Everyone charged with a criminal offence shall be presumed innocent until proved guilty according to law.

3

Everyone charged with a criminal offence has the following minimum rights:

a

to be informed promptly, in a language which he understands and in detail, of the nature and cause of the accusation against him;

b

to have adequate time and facilities for the preparation of his defence;

c

to defend himself in person or through legal assistance of his own choosing or, if he has not sufficient means to pay for legal assistance, to be given it free when the interests of justice so require;

d

to examine or have examined witnesses against him and to obtain the attendance and examination of witnesses on his behalf under the same conditions as witnesses against him;

e

to have the free assistance of an interpreter if he cannot understand or speak the language used in court.

Article 7
No punishment without law

1

No one shall be held guilty of any criminal offence on account of any act or omission which did not constitute a criminal offence under national or international law at the time when it was committed. Nor shall a heavier penalty be imposed than the one that was applicable at the time the criminal offence was committed.

2

This Article shall not prejudice the trial and punishment of any person for any act or omission which, at the time when it was committed, was criminal according to the general principles of law recognised by civilised nations.

Article 8
Right to respect for private and family life

1

Everyone has the right to respect for his private and family life, his home and his correspondence.

2

There shall be no interference by a public authority with the exercise of this right except such as is in accordance with the law and is necessary in a democratic society in the interests of national security, public safety or the economic well-being of the country, for the prevention of disorder or crime, for the protection of health or morals, or for the protection of the rights and freedoms of others.

Article 9
Freedom of thought, conscience and religion

1

Everyone has the right to freedom of thought, conscience and religion; this right includes freedom to change his religion or belief and freedom, either alone or in community with others and in public or private, to manifest his religion or belief, in worship, teaching, practice and observance.

2

Freedom to manifest one's religion or beliefs shall be subject only to such limitations as are prescribed by law and are necessary in a democratic society in the interests of public safety, for the protection of public order, health or morals, or for the protection of the rights and freedoms of others.

Article 10
Freedom of expression

1

Everyone has the right to freedom of expression. This right shall include freedom to hold opinions and to receive and impart information and ideas without interference by public authority and regardless of frontiers. This Article shall not prevent States from requiring the licensing of broadcasting, television or cinema enterprises.

2

The exercise of these freedoms, since it carries with it duties and responsibilities, may be subject to such formalities, conditions, restrictions or penalties as are prescribed by law and are necessary in a democratic society, in the interests of national security, territorial integrity or public safety, for the prevention of disorder or crime, for the protection of health or morals, for the protection of the reputation or rights of others, for preventing the disclosure of information received in confidence, or for maintaining the authority and impartiality of the judiciary.

Article 11
Freedom of assembly and association

1

Everyone has the right to freedom of peaceful assembly and to freedom of association with others, including the right to form and to join trade unions for the protection of his interests.

2

No restrictions shall be placed on the exercise of these rights other than such as are prescribed by law and are necessary in a democratic society in the interests of national security or public safety, for the prevention of disorder or crime, for the protection of health or morals or for the protection of the rights and freedoms of others. This Article shall not prevent the imposition of lawful restrictions on the exercise of these rights by members of the armed forces, of the police or of the administration of the State.

Article 12
Right to marry

Men and women of marriageable age have the right to marry and to found a family, according to the national laws governing the exercise of this right.

Article 14
Prohibition of discrimination

The enjoyment of the rights and freedoms set forth in this Convention shall be secured without discrimination on any ground such as sex, race, colour, language, religion, political or other opinion, national or social origin, association with a national minority, property, birth or other status.

Article 16
Restrictions on political activity of aliens

Nothing in Articles 10, 11 and 14 shall be regarded as preventing the High Contracting Parties from imposing restrictions on the political activity of aliens.

Article 17
Prohibition of abuse of rights

Nothing in this Convention may be interpreted as implying for any State, group or person any right to engage in any activity or perform any act aimed at the destruction of any of the rights and freedoms set forth herein or at their limitation to a greater extent than is provided for in the Convention.

Article 18
Limitation on use of restrictions on rights

The restrictions permitted under this Convention to the said rights and freedoms shall not be applied for any purpose other than those for which they have been prescribed.

Article 1
Protection of property

Every natural or legal person is entitled
to the peaceful enjoyment of his possessions.
No one shall be deprived of his possessions
except in the public interest and subject to
the conditions provided for by law and by the
general principles of international law.

The preceding provisions shall not, however,
in any way impair the right of a State to enforce
such laws as it deems necessary to control
the use of property in accordance with the general
interest or to secure the payment of taxes or
other contributions or penalties.

Article 2
Right to education

No person shall be denied the right to education.
In the exercise of any functions which it assumes
in relation to education and to teaching, the State
shall respect the right of parents to ensure
such education and teaching in conformity with
their own religious and philosophical convictions.

Article 3
Right to free elections

The High Contracting Parties undertake to hold
free elections at reasonable intervals by secret
ballot, under conditions which will ensure
the free expression of the opinion of the people
in the choice of the legislature.

Article 1
Abolition of the death penalty

The death penalty shall be abolished. No one shall
be condemned to such penalty or executed.

Article 2
Death penalty in time of war

A State may make provision in its law for
the death penalty in respect of acts committed in
time of war or of imminent threat of war; such
penalty shall be applied only in the instances
laid down in the law and in accordance with
its provisions. The State shall communicate to
the Secretary General of the Council of Europe
the relevant provisions of that law.

**To be read with Articles 16 to 18 of the
Convention.**

Good:
An introduction to ethics in graphic design
Section 3: Debating good/theory and practice
Lucienne Roberts +
Nigel Robinson illustration /**Lorna Fray** reader /
Malcolm Southward reader /**Rebecca Wright** reader

The continual shifts in focus of Charles and Ray Eames's fast-moving film **Powers of Ten** is reminiscent of life as a graphic designer. One minute the focus is micro – the exhaustive first meeting with a client – then macro as thousands of copies pour off a printing press en route to legions of people the designer will never meet. Common to all aspects of the practice, however, is interaction with other people.

Relationships are varied in type, intensity and scale; interests sometimes conflict. As Anthony Grayling observed on page 36:

…designers find themselves in a spider's web of duties – contractual duties, duties to clients, to stakeholders, to colleagues, to themselves and their work, and to society at large. It's sometimes difficult to serve everybody well while at the same time fulfilling one's implicit duties to society.

Roger Scruton wrote in his essay **Do the Right Thing**: 'It is not enough to be nice; you have to be good. We are attracted by nice people; but only on the assumption that their niceness is a sign of goodness'.[1] So, this section asks, what is the relationship between how we treat one another and being a good person, a good graphic designer and leading a good life?

The good life

The question, 'What is it that constitutes a good life?' was first asked by the Greeks in the fourth and fifth centuries BC. People are still struggling to find the answer today. From the pulpit to the market stall, voices proclaim what it is that makes a life 'good', while actors play out moral dilemmas and journalists pass judgements on our behalf.

What the question reveals is our quest to give life meaning. If you substitute 'good life' with 'worthwhile life' or 'valuable life', the profundity of the question becomes clear. By comparison, the modern interpretation of 'the good life' is a rather hedonistic and lightweight affair. The Greeks espoused the virtues of 'quality of life', but this encompassed ethereal and intellectual pleasures just as much as those of the flesh.

At first this might sound like advocacy for self-indulgence, but as Anthony Grayling explained in his essay **The Good Life**, 'When Socrates said "The life truly worth living is the considered life" he meant a life which is well informed, has worthwhile goals, and is lived discerningly so that one can respond to others well and live flourishingly for oneself'.[2] So, leading a good life does require us to consider others as well as ourselves.

We all struggle with alternative understandings of the good life – self-fulfilment versus self-sacrifice – but perhaps the ideal is that they work in tandem. Perri 6 and Ian Christie explore this idea further in their essay **On the Good Life**:

…the dreary conventional dichotomy between two meanings of the good life, between the pursuit of self-interested satisfaction, however enlightened, and the commitments of altruism and the 'ethical life', needs to be recast. Above the level of the satisfaction of basic needs, any reasonable conception of the good life involves both.[3]

for thoughts on…

→ **052**
Richard Holloway
on the Golden Rule

The Golden Rule

Awareness of ourselves, our feelings and aspirations is not a bad thing – it's the root of empathy. We don't need to have experienced something ourselves to imagine what we would feel if we were in a similar situation to someone else. With this comes an awareness of our impact on others.

This all sounds rather logical and predetermined, so where then is the goodness to be found in any action? Empathy is morally neutral – it doesn't tell us how to act, so goodness lies in what we choose to do with our awareness. This is where the Golden Rule comes in.

Almost all world religions and secular ethical philosophies agree on one principle: the Golden Rule, or ethic of reciprocity, that says 'treat others as you would wish to be treated in the same situation'. What this prescribes is consistency between our desires for ourselves and for others. The natural conclusion here is that differences in background, experience and ability do not have any bearing on our equal human rights.

Here are three examples of the many texts that espouse this belief:

Confucianism
Do not do to others what you do not want them to do to you.
Analects 15:23

Humanism
Treat other people as you'd want to be treated in their situation; don't do things you wouldn't want to have done to you.
British Humanist Association

Islam
No one of you is a believer until he desires for his brother that which he desires for himself.
40 Hadith of an-Nawawi 13

As a premise for ethical behaviour, how might this principle shape the practice of graphic design? Here are a few of the many ways it could be applied. They are based on the assumption that we are all well-adjusted people without conflicting agendas, which is obviously not always the case. Nevertheless, they are demonstrations of how fundamental the ethic of reciprocity would be to an ethical code of design practice.

Being polite

Underpinning the modern understanding of ethics is the idea that we are free individuals, able to make our own decisions and take responsibility for our actions. These ideas took shape during the eighteenth-century Enlightenment, when thinkers advocated applying reason to ethical decision-making – arguing that people were motivated to goodness not out of fear or superstition, but by a genuine sense of humanity.

The outward manifestation of this is being polite or having 'good' manners. Regardless of how genuine some of this might be, it is undeniably true that being on the receiving end of a 'please' or 'thank you' does make the world a more pleasant place.

Confucius, the early Eastern philosopher, argued that this is an indicator of how we consider others and that by adhering to a code of social etiquette, each of us plays a part in creating a more humane society. He highlighted five qualities that should be practised: courtesy, tolerance, faithfulness, diligence and kindness – something to try and remember, perhaps.

Plagiarism

Let's take plagiarism as one small indicator of the respect we have for other designers. Copyright law protects the intellectual property of designers, but sometimes the line between being inspired and blatant copying can be hard to establish.

Creative endeavour expresses something of the inner person, making plagiarism a form of violation. It's also stealing, so it must be 'wrong'. Imitation, however, is said to be the sincerest form of flattery, so work that obviously makes reference to others can be an homage – a mark of admiration and respect. The moral difference between the two may not be in the material outcome, but in the intention – whether one sets out to deceive.

Glossary of ethical thought

→ 066–068
Confucianism
Platonism
Aristotelianism
Epicureanism
Stoicism

Professionalism

If client and designer don't communicate their needs effectively, and are not mutually respectful, the resultant design is likely to be less successful. Professionals know this and yet have come to accept that the relationship is often confrontational. Why? It must be that each party misunderstands the objectives of the other, so here is an example of where better communication and a bit of empathy might help.

A common thread that runs through all the theoretical interviews in Section 2 is that behaving professionally is an ethical concern. This means that in accepting a commission we agree to do the job to the best of our abilities, on time and within budget. In exchange, we have the right to be paid as agreed and not to be hindered in our job. As Richard Holloway said on page 55:

In a sense there's a contract, a covenant between you and the people you're working for – obviously you don't want to cheat them, that's part of your ethic, you want to do the best for them. Maybe what you also need is an ethic of servant-hood, one based on the notion that helping other people is a good thing to do.

However, this is not a dispassionate exercise and even the most self-effacing designer injects a little bit of themselves into their work. In fact this is often the prerequisite to the work that the client requires. The apparent deal struck between client and graphic designer belies some of the requirements we designers really have. We want our clients to love us and, despite its generally ephemeral nature, we want our work to ensure some small degree of immortality. Love and death has a lot to do with creative endeavour. The problem is that many clients don't realise this.

So, clients need to tread a little more carefully in their comment and criticism – because it hurts – and designers need to understand that from their client's point of view, design is a small, but not invaluable, contribution to the world.

Inclusivity

Clients act as an interface between us and an unseen public, but their interests are not always the same as the public's. We are answerable to both, and at times it is necessary for us to represent the end-user in client discussions. An example of this might be in considering how to adhere to disability legislation. These laws enshrine the notion of access for all. This is obviously an ethical issue because the principle is that difference does not mean inequality – a standard fundamental to human rights.

The changes in European and American law, for example, are the culmination of years of campaigning and lobbying to realign opinions about how disability should be considered. This is best explained by contrasting the different perspectives of the medical and social models. The former places responsibility with the disabled person, the latter says the responsibility rests with society. So, for example, if a visually impaired person can't read a piece of public information because the type isn't big enough, the responsibility doesn't lie with them, but rather with society for not making sure that it can be read by everyone. This way of thinking is a demonstration of the Golden Rule in practice.

However, as with all ethical issues this isn't simple. For a start, how do we judge equality – by outcome or by chances offered? Given that we operate within a free market economy that encourages individual achievement and responsibility, it is equality of opportunity that most legislation seeks to establish.

Within graphic design there is debate around this subject. Most designers fear that in order to achieve access for all they will have to adhere to creatively restrictive guidelines. Clients meanwhile are anxious about the financial implications. Put crudely, larger type means more pages after all. All this could result in exclusion of a different kind: graphic design that may be highly legible, but is visually unsophisticated and unrefined. Does design that includes everyone exclude beauty and if so, is this 'right'?

The work ethic

In the previous examples we looked at how we treat clients and how they treat us, and how we think of the recipients of our work and our colleagues. But what about friends and family – our nearest and dearest?

In capitalist Western societies, being a workaholic is the only acceptable addiction. Working hard is deemed to have moral value. This 'work ethic' is derived from a puritan approach to life – one in which pleasure is regarded with suspicion and hard work is advocated as atonement for sins.

Most of us don't adhere consciously to these notions; we designers enjoy our work for a start. However, embedded somewhere in our subconscious is the feeling that working hard will result in almost divine rewards. Perhaps it's simply a 'vg gold star' sort of thing, left over from seeking approval at school. Whatever the psychological explanation, given the opportunity designers work extremely hard.

The process of producing work makes all creative people emotionally vulnerable. In graphic design 'being quiet' – or not having enough work – is tantamount to having 'failure' stamped on your forehead. Add even the slightest residue of the work ethic to a highly competitive and over-populated profession like graphic design, and what sort of behaviour is likely to be the result?

Speaking from personal experience I know that my other half thinks it best not to talk to me for some time after I get home – which is generally at some godforsaken hour of course. Why? Because I am self-obsessed, disengaged and oblivious to everyone else's needs – hardly fair to the person who will love and cherish me when all the clients have long since departed.

[1]
Roger Scruton
Do the Right Thing
in the Demos Collection
The Good Life
1998

[2]
AC Grayling
The Good Life in
The Heart of Things
Phoenix Press
2006

[3]
Perri 6 and Ian Christie
On the Good Life
in the Demos Collection
The Good Life
1998

Demos is an independent think-tank advocating everyday democracy.

When 'ethics' and 'graphic design' are put in the same sentence, inevitably two subjects come to mind. One is production methods – recycled paper et al – the other is the client. 'The client' is shorthand for 'the client's message'. So, this section considers how much the client's ethos, as depicted in their messages, need tally with your own.

The designer's remit

The first thing to remember is that we can't be responsible for everyone and everything all of the time. This is because we can't know everything all of the time. It is also because behaving ethically requires us to allow others freedom, within boundaries arrived at through some kind of common consent.

There is therefore a balance to be struck between social responsibility and individual freedom. Asking the question 'What if everybody did that?' is central to making ethical decisions. Even a small negative action can have prodigious consequences – what if we all dropped litter? So, in trying to behave ethically, the first thing has to be to consider our remit and areas of responsibility.

Although there are make or break situations that require us to stand by our principles, on the whole graphic design doesn't ask this of us. Instead we need to find an equilibrium between responsibilities to others and to ourselves, while remaining mindful of our roles as agents of a larger community. We have, for example, a responsibility to make the best use of our talents. This is a benefit to ourselves, to those who use our services and hopefully to the public at large. Being good is a complex business – it's not all about self-sacrifice.

This section examines how we choose to deploy our talents in the transmission of messages. This isn't about the message in a simple sense. The copy may say 'drink this coffee', which seems innocuous enough, but the way the coffee is made may make the message impossible to extol. There is no easy checklist to use in making these decisions, but here are some ways to start thinking about them.

Freedom of speech

Let's remind ourselves of some basics. Graphic designers are key players in the communication process because we give form to a message. Our job is to help make it travel further. It can be argued that in so doing we are effectively endorsing the message, and that therefore the decision to take on a particular job should be indicative of our own world-view – of what we think is 'right'.

But there are problems with this. Let us consider a crude example. Should you work on a campaign for the Conservatives if you vote Labour, the Republicans if you vote Democrat? Don't get sidetracked into considering the merits of each party. The question is, should you act as an advocate for opinions that are not your own and that you therefore believe to be 'wrong'?

A gut response might be 'no, you shouldn't' but, as Anthony Grayling pointed out on page 43, this position could reveal an objectionable attitude towards the rights of others. If we believe in freedom of speech, then shouldn't we encourage the representation of a diversity of views – even if we don't always agree with them? Is upholding these freedoms not more important than propagating our own world-view?

There are professions in which taking a completely objective position is a prerequisite. Jacqueline Roach talked on page 46 of the barrister's role in defending those who might be guilty – the justification is that everyone is innocent until proven otherwise and has the right to a defence. Delyth Morgan pointed out on page 62 that graphic designers have split loyalties to professionalism and artistry, which explains why they cannot apply such overarching professional principles:

It would be hard for a designer to approach this as objectively as a barrister… if a designer is working with a client without empathy for the issue, then I would imagine that could impede their ability to communicate effectively and creatively.

So a graphic designer's decision in this area is generally determined by personal conscience. This doesn't mean that it's impossible to arrive at some form of consensus, but initially each of us needs to decide where to draw the line. In so doing we will be defining a professional ethos.

Freedom of choice

It is our awareness of ourselves, and the impact that we have on others, that distinguishes humans from other creatures. A cat is pre-programmed to catch mice. It isn't conscious of its action, so cannot be held responsible for inflicting a form of torture. However, we are able to step outside ourselves. We feel empathy. We question the validity of our actions at the time of action and we have a memory of them, which means we can re-evaluate our actions and consider their consequences. This awareness enables us to make moral choices.

The notion of choice is therefore an essential component in the consideration of morality. Without freedom of choice you have no responsibility for your actions. The extent of these freedoms is open to debate. How much of our behaviour is impossible to change because it is determined by our genes, and by our psychological and physiological make-up? If you think 'most', then you may as well close this book, throw it in the recycling (if you are predetermined to do so) and have a cup of tea.

Most of us operate under the illusion of having freedom of choice. We can change in response to what we learn, witness and experience – and so within limitations we have a degree of choice. Since all decisions have an ethical dimension, our choices reflect our core values. So, every choice is potentially significant and meaningful… how empowering and yet simultaneously terrifying!

Glossary of ethical thought

→ 069, 070
Kantian ethics
Idealism

Social responsibility

'Mmm', you may be thinking, 'all decisions may have ethical repercussions, but in the grand scheme of things graphic design decisions can't be that important – surely'. Or, you may be thinking, 'Yes, I always knew graphic design had the potential to be the most important thing in the world and this book is about to confirm that. How fab'.

Neither position is true, because graphic design in itself is neutral – it becomes important by virtue of various things. For example, we designers often imbue our work with meaning over and above that required by the client or perceived by the end-user. Our work can be a form of artistic self-expression, a manifestation of political or religious belief, or an expression of social engagement. But for now let's concentrate on how our work impacts on other people and the resultant responsibility of the designer.

Swiss graphic designer Karl Gerstner said 'everything can be done consciously and seriously – or not',[1] by which he meant graphic design is as important as you choose to make it. The panoply that is loosely defined as graphic design includes the Gutenberg Bible, the London Underground map, a packet of Persil and all manner of other ephemeral and precious artefacts. These items are deemed more or less important because of their content, and the value we place on (in this case) seminal texts, information design or commerce. They can also be important because of their form, which can have some influence on how the content is interpreted. This loosely makes graphic design a political activity.

On page 62 Delyth Morgan made the connection between graphic design and politics clear:

...if you see your purpose as communicating a message, then you've got to have something to say. This inevitably means you have a perspective, which does make it a political activity. I guess the issues therefore revolve around context. Who you're working for, who you're trying to communicate with, and how you choose to do that, what kind of tools you use – even the kind of paper you use is a statement and that's before you even put anything on it.

Graphic design is fundamentally egalitarian; mass-produced, seen and used by everyone. Even the humblest of design jobs – bus tickets, newspapers, leaflets and packaging – can be approached with this at the forefront of your mind. As the early and mid-twentieth century architect Berthold Lubetkin famously said, 'nothing is too good for ordinary people'.

Of course it's not possible to maintain this level of idealism on every project. It's also humbling to remember that although graphic design affects everyone, this is usually subliminal. Nancy Bernard reminds us in her essay Reality Branding that in the contemporary Western world, most graphic design goes unnoticed:

The messages we deliver aren't that powerful – whether they're commercial or informational, people only care about them when they're actively looking for an LCD monitor or the way to San Jose. The rest of the time they're a kind of chattering background tappity-tap.[2]

Responsibility to persuade

Anthony Grayling pointed out on page 42 that graphic design is a rhetorical art; it is there to persuade. To be critical of it for being persuasive is like criticising a fisherman for catching fish. Clients will look to designers to put across their message most effectively and, having agreed to a commission, this is exactly what we should do.

However, before taking on any job we should obviously be mindful of what we are persuading people to do. We might, for example, not wish to participate in creating desires for things that people don't really want or need. Alternatively, we may see constant demand as a prerequisite to a successful capitalist society and argue that this is broadly for the good. It is up to each of us to decide where we feel it is 'right' to apply our commitment and skills.

Although form is not the focus of this section, the look of our work has a significant bearing on how a message is received. The choice of font, the crop of an image or the relative size of elements on the page can influence interpretation. This responsibility should not be undervalued. Form is also often the visual manifestation of a design ethos. The modernist approach to aesthetics is interesting in this regard. Modernism advocates aesthetic neutrality: messages presented as transparently as possible, with design intervention kept to a minimum. The ethical argument for this is obvious: design should be a facilitator in conveying messages, but should not be part of the message itself.

for thoughts on...

→ 060
Delyth Morgan
on collective responsibility

→ 133
Chris de Bode
on truth

→ 137, 138
Sheila Levrant de Bretteville
on socially engaged work

→ 185
Pat Kahn
on useless design

The counter argument is that this is impossible to achieve, and that trying to conceal the role of design in persuasion is nothing short of lying. As the British designer Neville Brody said:

I felt it was key to reveal the involvement of the human hand in the process of delivering idea A to destination B... the reader [should] be very aware that someone had been involved in interpreting the idea... I've recognised that the process of communication is a dialogue, not a monologue. I'm not dictating, I'm part of the message that I'm transporting.[3]

Conflicting principles

For most of us, our ethical decision-making has something to do with striking a balance between living life to the full and not harming others. This sounds simple, but the detail of each situation will be different, subtle and shifting. Thinking about ethics requires us to welcome complexity and to be constantly asking questions of ourselves and of others.

We need to be well-informed and apply objectivity so that decisions are not determined by prejudice and bias. We need to be open to ideas such as the view that to work for obviously 'nice' organisations might not always be the most effective way to make a difference. As Jacqueline Roach said on page 47, 'isn't it better not to walk away from jobs on ethical grounds, but to ask if there's some way that you can have influence, something you can bring?'.

This essay has focused on our responsibility to the wider world and the recipients of our work, but there are other immediate and conflicting responsibilities too. It's not difficult to refuse work if you are financially secure, but being principled can be an unaffordable luxury. The multifarious responsibilities that we all have can sometimes conflict. German designer Erik Spiekermann points out that ethical theory and practice don't always concur: 'faced with the decision to sack ten people or take on a job for an evil empire, I'm not going to sack ten people'.[4] So, do you make decisions on the basis of a set of immovable principles, or assess the 'rightness' of an action on the basis of its outcomes alone?

[1]
Lucienne Roberts
Drip-dry Shirts
AVA
2005

[2]
Nancy Bernard
Reality Branding: Addressing Real Concerns and Real Needs in
Citizen Designer: Perspectives on Design Responsibility
Allworth Press
2003

[3]
[4]
Jonathan Baldwin/ Lucienne Roberts
Visual Communication
AVA
2006

Glossary of ethical thought

→ 068
Stoicism

→ 070
Marxism

Debating good

Who should I work for?   092 : 093

Is it okay to be happy?/essay

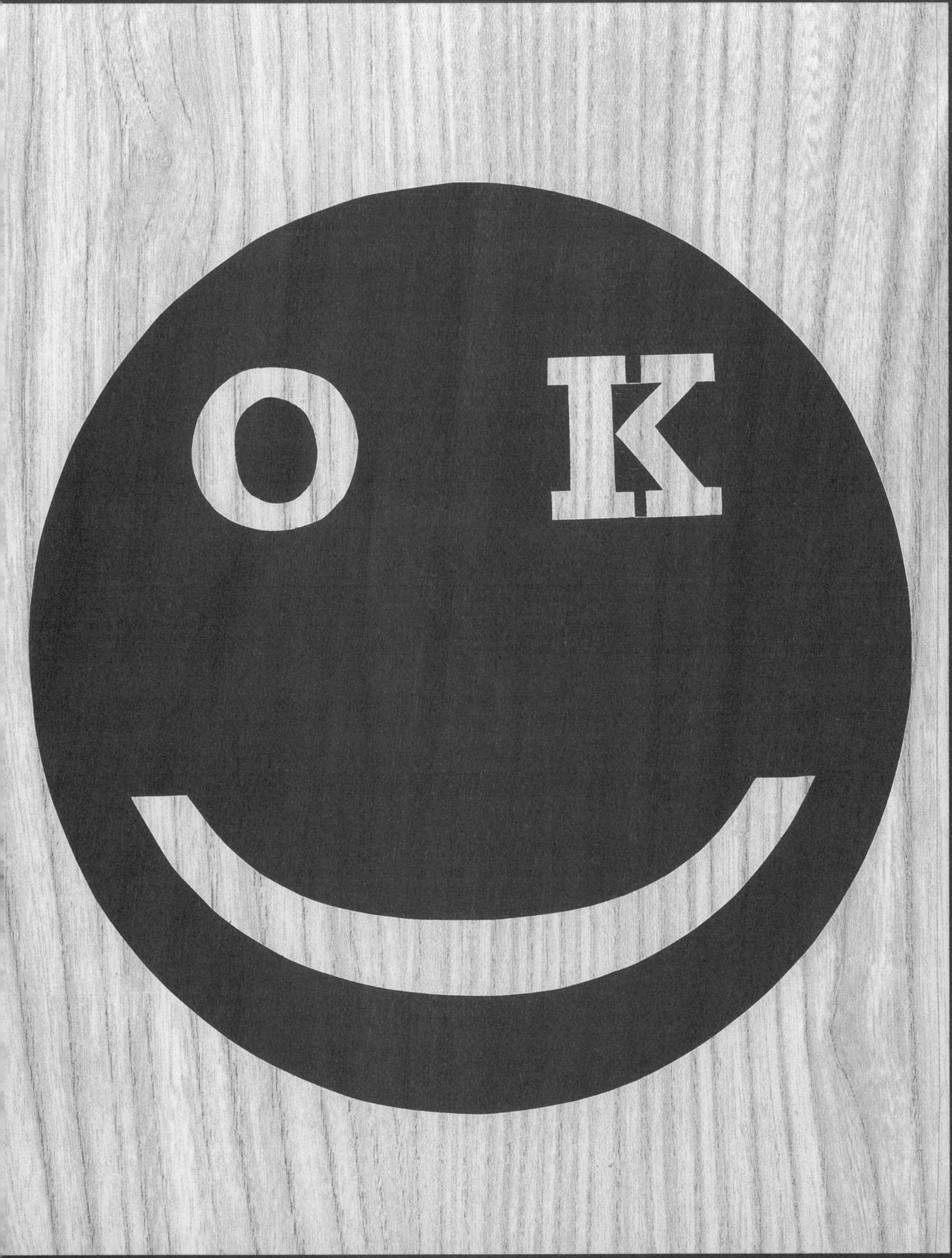
O K

In the previous essays we looked at ethics in relation to our impact on other people. The focus of this section is happiness – and that includes our own, not in order to encourage self-indulgence, but because as Anthony Grayling said on page 37, 'if you want to live a good life, and to do good in the world, you've got to be good to yourself'.

In his essay On Work and Happiness Alain de Botton explored the contemporary schism between the expectations of what work can deliver and the reality. 'The most remarkable feature of the modern workplace has nothing to do with computers, automation and globalisation. It lies in the widely-held belief that work should make us happy.'[1]

De Botton however does cite artistic endeavour as an example of work that can deliver a kind of happiness – it is stimulating, to some degree self-expressive and therefore self-defining. Graphic design is a hybrid art form. There are multiple stakeholders in graphic design, rendering compromise inevitable. It can sometimes feel quite an arduous business as a result, but nevertheless the joys of a well-kerned heading, a perfectly printed page or a dynamic layout are hard to surpass. So, the focus of this section is happiness – our own and that which we can bring to others.

Happiness and its relationship to ethics

Aristotle crucially identified happiness as an end in itself, and the ultimate goal of human pursuits. He held that it is natural to humans to seek happiness and fundamental to how they make choices in life. This is why happiness is crucial to ethics.

As we will see, Aristotle's concept of happiness is far more inclusive than that of the utilitarians, who tended to identify happiness with simple pleasurable sensation. Present-day synonyms range from 'cheerfulness' to 'contentment' and 'ecstasy', but Aristotle's notion of happiness was rather more profound than some of these indicate. He gave it the name 'eudaimonia', which means 'a flourishing state of the soul'. This sounds rather ethereal. In one sense it is, in that Aristotle saw the highest ideal of a good life as contemplation. However, he meant this ideal to involve physical and emotional as well as intellectual engagement in the world. He also placed great emphasis on 'practical wisdom' and reasoned behaviour, proposing that doing what is right is often the midpoint between extremes – such as generosity instead of meanness or profligacy.

Quality of life and beauty

The Greeks placed great store by quality of life and the role that art can play in this. Quality of life could be associated as much with state of mind as physical experience, but an understanding and appreciation of art was one way of transcending to this place. Many of us will identify with this claim and say that happiness is achieved as a result of this process. Through engagement with art we are taken 'out of ourselves', living in the moment and yet travelling far and wide in our imaginations to make some kind of blissful sense of life. This can be understood from the famous last lines of John Keats's Ode on a Grecian Urn:

'Beauty is truth, truth beauty,' – that is all
Ye know on earth, and all ye need to know.[2]

The term 'beauty' is a bit of a problem though, because notions of what is beautiful are varied – if not contradictory – and very rarely universally held. Anthony Grayling suggested on page 39 that it might be helpful to list associated words – eye-catching, imaginative, uplifting, striking and so on – in order to arrive at a shared understanding of the term.

for thoughts on...

→ 038–040
Anthony Grayling
on happiness, beauty and
quality of life

→ 054, 055
Richard Holloway
on hybrid art forms

→ 134
Chris de Bode
on compromise

→ 138
Sheila Levrant de Bretteville
on self-obsession

If this list is expansive and exhaustive enough, then it is fair to say that most graphic designers want to produce 'beautiful' work and that this makes us profoundly happy. Although our practice is grounded in commerce and the requirements of a brief, it can still deliver joy and delight and certainly can enhance the quality of life for all concerned. As Anthony Grayling said on page 39: 'design, which can so richly enhance the beauty of the world, is thereby adding to the spiritual value of the world'. On page 54 Richard Holloway drew a parallel between architects and graphic designers:

You're probably more like architects than autonomous visual artists. In many ways this is one of the most influential art forms. I think the grace and beauty of public space can help to civilise people, just as ugly public space can brutalise them. …There is an ethic in design that works well and is aesthetically enriching.

Self-expression and compromise

This is all well and good until we hit the thorny area of self-expression. Clients rarely employ a graphic designer purely on the basis of their unique artistic voice. Our clients do not usually see themselves as patrons of the arts and so for designers to treat them as such, without their knowledge or consent, is an act of deception – and surely 'wrong'.

The ideal is to build relationships with clients that are truly simpatico, so that the client needs what we naturally do best. However, being ethical requires us to recognise the rights of others to have an opinion, even if it is contrary to our own. This involves holding some tensions between self-fulfilment and the effect we have on others – compromising our desires is sometimes appropriate and inevitable.

Compromise may also alleviate the odd twinge of guilt. Most of us feel uneasy focusing solely on our own happiness when there is so much suffering in the world. This of course is a fruitless by-product of empathy if it doesn't provoke some kind of action – after all it doesn't alleviate the pain of others to be in pain also. But according to the ethic of reciprocity, to desire happiness for oneself is a step towards desiring it for others too, and so can be seen as a step towards behaving ethically so long as it is kept in check.

Glossary of ethical thought

→ 067
Aristotelianism

The absence of suffering

A few years ago Woody Allen gave a talk at London's National Film Theatre in which he described his work as a 'quality distraction' from the incessant existential angst of asking 'Why am I here?'. Work absorbs him so much that he has no time to ask the questions that may cause him pain. Graphic design can have the same function. This is why being busy is so vital for many of us. Our work brings a happiness of sorts that could be defined more accurately as an absence of pain – an idea central to ethics and philosophy.

In 2003 research from both the University of Wisconsin and the University of California San Francisco Medical Centre in the USA suggested that Buddhists are often happier than other people. Parts of the brain associated with good moods and positive feelings were found to be more active in Buddhists. Studies also suggest that meditation helps Buddhists deal better with anger and fear.

The second Noble Truth of Buddhism is that the root of suffering can be defined as a craving for, or clinging to, the wrong things. So acquisitiveness and searching for stability in this constantly shifting world, results in unhappiness. One objective of meditation is to free oneself from habitual states of mind like greed and delusion that cause us to suffer. The third Noble Truth is that 'nirvana' – freedom from suffering – is possible.

Wow – this is a relief. Self-worth can start from within. Reputation of course is important to us all. But we are so vulnerable to the shifting opinions of others – how wonderful to be freed from superficial judgements based on acquisitions, monetary or otherwise. Happiness indeed!

Boredom and power

The philosopher Arthur Schopenhauer also identified happiness as an absence of suffering. He took a fatalistic approach. He considered that we do not have control over many of our circumstances and argued that desire is a source of pain because it makes us see our present situation as lacking in some way. He concluded, however, that if we feel no desire we are also dissatisfied because we are 'bored'. By this he meant that we feel a different absence, that of desiring.

Friedrich Nietzsche took this idea further, arguing that since when we are bored we say we have nothing to do, rather than nothing to desire, the boredom stems from wanting desires because they give us something to do. We also feel bored when we are engaged in unchallenging pursuits, so Nietzsche argued that we desire resistance in our activities so that we can feel empowered when this is overcome.

It is easy to see how Nietzsche's theories relate to the practice of graphic design. The brief is the resistance described. There is undoubtedly great satisfaction to be had from solving any design problem. This may be from developing hierarchical typographic systems, or from constructing secondary meanings by juxtaposing a set of images. The important thing is the resultant sense of achievement and empowerment, albeit temporary, that is as Nietzsche described.

The bigger picture

Happiness can also be derived from focusing on others instead of oneself. As you might expect, Buddhism is useful on this one too. Buddhists believe that everything is interconnected and that once seen in this way, the 'self' becomes less important because it is a transient part of a much bigger whole.

This idea of interconnection is a natural by-product of graphic design work. We are always aware of the needs of our clients and end-users. To do our job properly, and to communicate with others effectively, we must become engrossed in their worlds and problems. We can become so absorbed that self-awareness does momentarily cease. This can be a humbling and simultaneously elevating process. We can also learn from our clients, and as Plato said, there is great pleasure to be had from expanding the mind.

The utilitarian nature of graphic design can therefore result in personal fulfilment that is not focused on the self. It makes us feel good to put our professional skills to good use. Working in the voluntary or public sectors, for example, may bring aesthetic limitations, but by virtue of the messages being conveyed we feel validated because we are contributing to a bigger endeavour.

The utilitarian approach

The British school of utilitarianism founded by Jeremy Bentham was famous for its principle of 'the greatest happiness to the greatest number'. Bentham observed that individuals seek happiness over pain, so the resultant happiness of any action was the way to judge whether it was 'good'. He argued that ethically speaking happiness should be maximised for the many – in a sense this is the Golden Rule meets collective responsibility.

This sounds wonderfully straightforward. Part of this simplicity derives from the fact that early utilitarians envisaged happiness in terms of units of pleasurable feeling which could simply be added up and 'maximised'. However, broader conceptions of happiness are less amenable to utilitarian calculation. Happiness can be the outcome of all manner of human activity, and it is not clear that there is any single pleasurable feeling common to them all. If a broader, Aristotelian, idea of happiness is acknowledged, utilitarianism loses some of its apparent straightforwardness. There is also a risk that to always sanction the happiness of the majority could lead to a form of philistine mob rule. This would put in jeopardy that which designers hold dear – the right to individual self-expression.

Utilitarianism requires us to consider actions in terms of the anticipated results. This isn't an exact science because the addition of time can lead to unexpected outcomes. It may be that what you do now causes pain, but you know that in the long term it will have the reverse effect – the 'cruel to be kind' idea if you like. The converse might also be true. However, the basic idea of utilitarianism, that we should consider what might be of universal benefit, is of course a sound one that still resonates today.

So, yes it is okay to be happy. In fact, being ethical requires that we strive to be so.

[1]
Alain de Botton
On Work and Happiness in
On Seeing and Noticing
Penguin Books Ltd
2005

[2]
John Keats
Ode on a Grecian Urn
May 1819 in
The Norton Anthology
of Poetry
Norton
1983

Glossary of ethical thought

→ 069, 070, 071
Utilitarianism
Idealism
Nietzsche

Debating good   **Is it okay to be happy?**   098 : 099

Judging and being judged is an uncomfortable part of being a graphic designer. Like lambs to the slaughter, we present ideas to our clients, enter competitions and seek inclusion in trade magazines. We look for approval, but are understandably disdainful of what is a subjective and potentially undermining process. Having been judged, designers are often the worst offenders when it comes to openly and honestly assessing other designers' work. Designers are no more nasty than anyone else, but the value systems available are so various and changeable that objectivity and consistency seem almost impossible to achieve.

However, no book about ethics and graphic design can avoid the subject of judgement because terms like 'good' and 'bad', and 'right' and 'wrong' have the notion of value embedded within them. This section looks at the conflicts in ethical thinking that are central to debates about value in design.

Moral language

The lack of an adequate language with which to make judgements is the heart of the problem. There is no consensus for example about what 'good' design means. This recognition of the inadequacy of moral language did not of course start with design. In the early twentieth century various thinkers and philosophers claimed that moral language was universally meaningless. Language, it was said, can only accurately express empirical facts.

The emotivists argued that moral language only describes individual preference. So, when someone describes an object as 'good', what they mean is that they like it; a 'bad' action is one that, under similar circumstances, they would not do. Put simply, moral language is nothing more than subjectivity writ large. This is an extreme kind of relativism and its lack of objectivity might seem to render value judgements null and void.

Even today this is all rather shocking. It is also perhaps not very useful. Most of us are more comfortable with the idea that we share some basic moral values, that your 'good' is the same, or at least similar, to mine. As Perri 6 and Ian Christie point out in their essay **On the Good Life**, it is impossible to make changes for the better without this shared understanding of what 'good' means:

Tackling social policy problems cannot simply be about 'non-judgemental' measures and debates about inputs and outputs of resources. It must also be about good outcomes, and the prevention of ills; and these are bound up with arguments over what counts as 'good'.[1]

That said, developing a broad set of terms with which to describe – and therefore judge – graphic design would be a useful thing. Explaining and justifying design work objectively protects it from the vagaries of personal preference. On page 41 Anthony Grayling suggested a set of alternative words to replace 'good' that might include 'effective', 'striking' or 'accessible', for example.

for thoughts on...

→ 036
Anthony Grayling on definitions of the well-intentioned designer

→ 041
Anthony Grayling on value in design

→ 117
Michael Marriott on design language

On page 54 Richard Holloway considered whether there is a difference between intrinsic and instrumental goods in the arts. In other words, work can be good because it is conceptually or aesthetically groundbreaking or because it has some other benefit to society at large. These distinctions recognise that art and design can have a value other than in pure terms. You might think the latter more relevant to this book, but ethics is concerned with quality of life, so all aspects of design have an ethical dimension.

Developing a language that allows us to draw distinctions between different versions of 'good' design not only more truly reflects the diversity of the practice, but also allows for greater inclusion. As Delyth Morgan said on page 60: 'I understand that without feelings of self-worth... it is hard to carry on and so understandably we seek approval from many sources'.

The discomfort of judging

The inexactitude of language is not the only problem in making judgements though. Central to living an ethical life is the belief that we are all equal and each have the right to be respected and valued as such. In the modern world the freedom of the individual is all-important. We don't like being told what to do and question the right of those passing judgement. Conversely, we want to live our lives with a good conscience and so look for mechanisms to facilitate this taking place. Embedded within these conflicting needs and desires are the two extreme philosophies that inform many judgements of design: relativism and absolutism.

Thinking relatively

The relativist position is that there are no moral absolutes and that there is no one truth because standards of 'good' and 'bad', and 'right' and 'wrong' are related to circumstance or to the society or individual that adopts them. Although relativism is generally thought of as a twentieth century idea it was the Greek philosopher Protagoras who said 'man is the measure of all things'.[2] This is usually interpreted to mean that the individual human being, rather than a god or a set of moral laws, is the ultimate giver of value.

In design terms, postmodernism is related to relativism. It embraces diversity, welcomes ambiguity and rejects rigid dogma and design intolerance. It celebrates irony because nothing, particularly absolute authority, is beyond question or to be wholly revered.

The result of this way of thinking is that a design project cannot be deemed good or bad in itself. It can be said to be good or bad when considered against the circumstances that created it, or by applying a variety of different criteria. By this means, different value judgements of the same piece of work are possible. It is equally valid, for example, to argue that the design of a cigarette packet is 'good' if it sells more cigarettes and 'bad' because it promotes a potentially harmful activity. It's all down to how you look at it – and each opinion is equally valid in a relativist world.

As an intellectual exercise this is interesting, but critics argue that relativism is useless as a vehicle through which to direct change, and results in a kind of moral and aesthetic free-for-all. But, as Anthony Grayling pointed out on page 41, expressions of difference are legitimate. Designers have to recognise that the converse of their work having value and impact is that it can cause disquiet or be unsettling, and that people have the right to say so.

The way forward is to widen design language so that discussions about relative worth are not simply forays into prejudice and narrow-mindedness. A resounding success of relativism has certainly been greater tolerance and a respect for each individual's view. The negative side of this is the focus on the rights of 'I' as opposed to 'we'. At risk is the demise of the notion of social responsibility, coupled with a hideous preoccupation with the self.

Glossary of ethical thought

→ 072
Emotivism

Elitism

Seen against this framework, the idea of an elite is rightly abhorrent. However, are we really to believe that all opinions are equal? How can we meaningfully teach anything if all values are a matter of personal choice? Geoff Mulgan puts in a plea not for privilege per se, but for the approbation of excellence:

We need to leave behind the terror of judgement that has made being 'judgemental' a cardinal sin in an age of popular sovereignty, multiculturalism and consumer choice. The truth is that we can make some judgements about the goodness of lives: not only their ethical qualities, but also aesthetic ones, how much sense, meaning, coherence they have; how much a life is fulfilled; how much a life leaves a legacy. These judgements will often be contested, and the capacity to make judgements should never again be monopolised by an elite or a priestly caste. But it is not true that all lives are equal, any more than all art is equal. There are enduring distinctions to be drawn between the good and the bad, the excellent and the mediocre. Great works of art can still communicate and still overpower our senses, just as great lives, in all their myriad forms, can still inspire us, and just as good technologies enrich our lives, and stretch our capacities, whereas bad ones leave us docile and unsatisfied.[3]

Unintentionally, relativism panders to the philistine. As Jeanette Winterson argues in her essay **Art Objects**, without a respect for experience and education, all artistic endeavour can be denounced as elitist tosh:

We hear a lot about the arrogance of the artist but nothing about the arrogance of the audience. The audience, who have not done the work, who have not taken any risks, whose life and livelihood are not bound up at every moment with what they are making, who have given no thought to the medium or the method, will glance up, flick through, chatter over the opening chords, then snap their fingers and walk away like some monstrous Roman tyrant.[4]

Belief in absolutes

At the other end of the judgement spectrum to relativism is absolutism, hard to envision without a backdrop of scenes from **Triumph of the Will** or Stalinist propaganda. Perhaps a better way to start is by considering the benefits of having a few rules. On page 48 the barrister Jacqueline Roach argued that without rules, arrived at through common consent, we feel less valuable because assessment of our worth is only subjective. Ironically dictatorships, associated with rules in the extreme, often come about because of the insecurities engendered by not having enough of a structure in the first place. 'Being told that anything goes can make you feel valueless... When people are feeling in a state of crisis they want certainty. This is why certain iniquitous societies have flourished – Nazism for example.'

Believing in the human capacity for reason and the absolute nature of rationality, philosophers have advocated that a rational analysis of the world will deliver absolute ethical codes. The resultant theories, such as natural law and utilitarianism, have sought to establish frameworks in which speaking of good/bad and right/wrong does become meaningful. Central to these ideas is a belief not so much in the individual, but in the collective good.

for thoughts on...

→ 053
**Richard Holloway
on tolerance**

→ 061
**Delyth Morgan
on dogma**

In design terms, modernism is related to these beliefs. It embraces rationality and reason, believing that the correct analysis of the design problem will naturally result in a right solution. It advocates minimal design intervention so that communication is clear and effective. It is utopian, harnessing mass production in a mission to democratise through design and make the world a better place. In short, modernism sought to ally logic with a humanising design agenda.

Modernism tried to find order in a chaotic world. To do this it had rules. Not of the 'thou shalt range left' variety, but rather it said 'design should reflect its time, the job it is there to do and the materials with which it is made'.

Critics say this is the manifestation of a reductive approach to life – that modernism gave answers because questions make us feel insecure. By proposing some kind of absolute 'truth', modernists were criticised for having evangelical and dictatorial tendencies. As Richard Holloway said on page 52, big ideas can be dangerous. If the principle becomes more important than the outcome we can lose sight of the potentially damaging results of our actions.

Although not directly prescribed, modernist principles generally result in a form of aesthetic minimalism. This has also been criticised as formulaic, sterile and resulting in abstract solutions accessible only to the educated few.

As we have seen, ways of thinking about judging goodness in design are multifarious and inconclusive. However, the answer to the question posed is clear: everyone has the right to judge, but some judgements are more right than others.

[1]
Perri 6 and Ian Christie
On the Good Life
in the Demos Collection
The Good Life
1998

[2]
This quotation is recapitulated in Plato's
Theaetetus

[3]
Geoff Mulgan
Timeless Values
in the Demos Collection
The Good Life
1998

[4]
Jeanette Winterson
Art Objects in
Art Objects:
Essays on Ecstasy
and Effrontery
Vintage
1996

Glossary of ethical thought

→ 070
Idealism

→ 073
Ethics of difference

Debating good   **Who has the right to judge?**   104 : 105

Graphic design has become a highly competitive, dog-eat-dog kind of profession, reflecting society's shift in focus over the last 30 years from collective to individual responsibility. It relies on voracity in order to survive. It engenders insecurity, envy and greed in its practitioners and promotes acquisitiveness and waste in other people. So far these essays have been rather idealistic in tone, with their talk of beauty and happiness, artistic and political utopias. There hasn't been too much finger pointing or judgement going on – just a kindly 'you can look at it like this or like that' kind of approach. But here comes the gloomy prognosis for our ethical condition. This essay asks what design is really worth – and that doesn't just mean monetarily.

Individualism and behaving badly

Designers are a pretty idiosyncratic bunch. Operating in an entrepreneurial climate probably suits most of us. In order to survive at all, practising designers have to be self-motivated and self-believing. The economics of the free market with its minimal state intervention and focus on individual freedom should really be right up our street.

But graphic design falls between two stools – profession one minute, vocation the next. It means that many of us oscillate between running a business – with a keen eye on the bottom line – and a studio, where the value of work is not commensurate with fees charged. Graphic designers often work for themselves or in small groups. There are no basic ground rules about work practices that can be referred to by practitioners and the result is that designers are unprotected. Delyth Morgan said on page 60, 'I believe that we are better served by being part of a community and helping each other, than as individuals fighting for our own turf' so, perhaps an old-fashioned trade union would not be such a bad idea.

Supply and demand, it is argued, determine all. However, there seems to be an inconsistency in this regard between design education and practice. Although there is a value in education for its own sake, design is currently an over-populated business, so many talented graduates are unemployed. You can argue that this is how the free market works. It is self-levelling – which is an innocuous way of saying that lots of designers simply won't survive – but added competition also contributes to a growth in unethical work practices. In design, the prevalence of unpaid competitive pitching is just one example of this.

When people are insecure and frightened they are also more likely to behave badly. We designers lie all the time. We say 'yes' to deadlines we can't meet – safe in the knowledge that clients are always so late themselves that it will become their fault. We secretly mark up suppliers' services because we don't think we can earn enough otherwise.

On page 55 Richard Holloway cited envy as the worst of all sins:

Of course really big, secure people are not posturing all the time, they do not always have to assert their creativity. There are some astonishingly gifted people. That's where envy comes in, which is sorrow at another's good. It's not even a kind of avarice, where you want what the other person has – envy is when a person has a gift and does something good and that makes you sad. This makes it the meanest sin in the book.

Oops, we don't fare too well on this one either. As with most creative industries, jealousies run high in the design business. These are generally to do with accreditation of what is called 'good' work, even though we haven't developed a language with which to adequately discuss this notion.

The designer as author

Perhaps what is called for is a bit of humility, coupled with a reminder that self-absorption can make us absurd. During the last 20 years this absurdity seems to have reached new heights. Michael Rock's article **The Designer as Author** is an exhaustive examination of what this concept might mean. He concludes:

While some claims for authorship may be as simple as a renewed sense of responsibility, at times they seem to be ploys for property rights, attempts to finally exercise some kind of agency where there has traditionally been none. Ultimately the author = authority. The longing for graphic authorship may be the longing for a kind of legitimacy, or a kind of power, that has so long eluded the obedient designer. But do we get anywhere by celebrating the designer as some central character? Isn't that what fueled the last 50 years of design history? If we really want to move beyond the designer-as-hero model of history, we may have to imagine a time when we can ask 'What difference does it make who designed it?'.[1]

Inequality and unhappiness

One of the problems with individualism and the resultant competitive spirit is that it fosters inequality, which runs contrary to much ethical thinking. If you take the utilitarian advocacy of the 'greatest happiness to the greatest number' as a starting point, it doesn't take long to arrive at Karl Marx, the redistribution of wealth and 'from each according to his ability, to each according to his needs'.[2]

However, the current debate around equality is focused on the unhappiness that extreme disparity brings. From an economic point of view, the Centre-Left argue that it doesn't matter if the gap between rich and poor is increasing, so long as the poor are becoming better off. Will Hutton contends that this argument is flawed as happiness doesn't rest with what we own:

...the human experience is essentially social. We do not live as islands; we seek and offer each other's good opinion as the basic fuel of human intercourse. The expectation and need for reciprocity is a more generalised human need; it underpins friendship and trust. It is at the core of our conceptions of social capital without which our societies begin to become unhinged... Building friendships becomes harder between people whose status and income varies hugely; and friendship is a basic emotional need.[3]

The happiness of a designer is not often tied to wealth, but it is linked to status of a different kind. We need to be clear about where our value lies. As Richard Holloway observed on page 55, 'I understand that there's a conflict, because artists often want to be prophetic individuals, but I suspect that a lot of what makes design valuable isn't that it is unique or pioneering'. A more inclusive notion of 'good' design would result in a more open and tolerant design community and engender greater equality and therefore happiness. It might also result in more useful graphic design.

Being good citizens of the world

Restlessness is, however, at the heart of how our economy works. We graphic designers are simultaneously tortured by it and propagating it. As Richard Holloway said on page 57:

The whole nature of the market is to increase discontent. There's something deeply flawed about it. On the other hand people say it's that discontent that's made us the most creative animals on the planet. As well as despoiling the planet we painted the Sistine Chapel, we built St Peter's in Rome and St Paul's in London, and York Minster – it's all part of the same package in a way.

But if a designer's first impulse is to keep making things, is this fast becoming unsustainable? In little more than 100 years, designers have gone from promoting craft and humane approaches to manufacture, to celebrating the democratising benefits of mass production, embracing the brand and the creativity demanded by have-it-now/throw-it away booms. But this cannot go on.

Designers are trained to solve problems and know that answers don't lie in unquestioningly producing more. Manifestos like First Things First 2000 and the huge success of Naomi Klein's book No Logo are testament to this awareness. Designers are happy to test the status quo.

In his essay Runaway World, David Goldblatt argued for a realignment of ideas about where quality and happiness lie. This could be of enormous benefit to designers:

First, environmentalists have argued that the simple equation between abundance and the good life is flawed. Abundance and affluence bring their own problems. A good life is something greater than the sum of what we can manage to consume before we die. This is a rich if under-worked seam for a politics of the good life that is based on the qualitative texture of experience rather than the quantitative accumulation of things... we will only curb our voracious environmental appetites and have the opportunity to cultivate alternative sources of the good life if we are prepared collectively and individually to re-evaluate the meaning of wealth and well-being.[4]

for thoughts on...

→ 056, 057
Richard Holloway
on the free market

→ 063
Delyth Morgan
on inequality and
unhappiness

→ 116–117
Michael Marriott
on capitalism and
sustainability

→ 162–173
Sustainability Issue Mapping

The blame, if you like, lies with us all. In the over-abundant West we don't even pay properly for essentials, like food. Cheap must surely be best, because it means we can buy more. Sustainability may be forced upon us, but the result is likely to be a better quality of life. Our understanding of value for money needs to be reconfigured. This isn't about buying nothing, but it is about buying less and paying and valuing it more. It also requires us to share, as Julian Baggini argued in a recent newspaper article in the Guardian:

The value whose time may have come now is not one that obviously springs to mind when making a list of great virtues. But, when you consider its history and pedigree, it seems obvious that what the world needs now is not love, sweet love, but simply to share. Sharing looks like the antidote to all the evils that weigh on the minds of guilt-ridden westerners: greed, excessive individualism, inequality and environmental destruction. All these problems would vanish, so it seems, if only we could learn to share more.[5]

Richard Holloway argued on page 56 that perhaps it is time for designers to define themselves less via their work and more as citizens of the world:

The market is a glorious thing, but it is also a monster that devours its children. Many of us, designers included, have to admit to being prostitutes in that sense – selling a talent on behalf of this great monster, the most terrifyingly powerful thing on the globe. Maybe the answer is not to deal with it through your art, but to take an interest in the politics and philosophy of the market. Maybe it's as citizens you should be asking these questions. Okay we serve this thing that is good at delivering Reebok shoes and interesting coffee and cheeses, but it is also capable of despoiling the environment and flattening complete cultures, so maybe we should be critically interested in the thing we're serving.

So, being ethical requires that we remember we are people first and designers second.

[1]
Michael Rock
The Designer as Author
in Eye magazine
number 20, spring 1996

[2]
Karl Marx
Critique of the Gotha Programme
1875

[3]
Will Hutton
Do We Mind the Gap?
in the Demos Collection
The Good Life
1998

[4]
David Goldblatt
Runaway World
in the Demos Collection
The Good Life
1998

[5]
Julian Baggini
Common Sense
in the Guardian
25 March 2006

These five essays take the theory explored
in Section 2 as a starting point and test it
from a graphic design perspective. Ethics is
all about shades of grey. To develop a set of
dos and don'ts is impossible, but some kind of
consensus can be reached.

Broadly the conclusion so far is that
graphic design can be 'good' by virtue of its
content, its form or both. However, behaving
ethically requires good intentions as well
as outcomes. So, for example, despite
the endemic competitiveness of the business,
it is not worth letting consideration
of others wane amid a flurry of selfishly
driven creativity.

This doesn't mean self-sacrifice is always
necessary. Happiness, including your own,
is a prerequisite of good design. Constant
altruism will result in bitterness and
despondency. A balance needs to be struck –
more greys – between work that engenders
some personal fulfilment for us and work
that gives pleasure or is useful to the end-
user. Being a designer can make us happy by
virtue of being useful to our clients and the
community at large. It can also bring ethereal
or intellectual rewards. Our work can be
beautiful or give delight. All these aspects of
graphic design have an ethical dimension.

Graphic design is a political activity.
It gives form to messages. Designers have
to consider the value of the message,
and the form it takes. They also have to ask
whether they have a role in inducing desires
that can never be sated, that may result in
profound discontent and contribute to
waste and environmental destruction on an
unprecedented scale. For graphic designers,
the tactile pleasures of ink on paper are
crucial to making a design a success, so it is
hard to accept that electronic publications
may be less wasteful. These environmental
concerns will form the next problem that
designers must help to solve.

Good:
An introduction to ethics in graphic design
Section 4: Being good/practitioner experience
Lucienne Roberts/Rebecca Wright +
Michael Marriott/Paula Scher/
Oded Ezer/Divya Chadha/Billie Tsien/
Will Holder/Simon Esterson/
thomas.matthews/James Victore/
Chris de Bode/Deborah Szebeko/
Sheila Levrant de Bretteville/Ali Rashidi/
Luba Lukova/Susanne Dechant

Michael Marriott spent his
childhood designing and making things and
studied at the London College of Furniture
and the Royal College of Art in England before
starting his own studio in 1993. Marriott is
interested in the essential nature of things,
and designs detailed functional household
objects and furniture, celebrated for their
elegance and ingenuity. He has designed
furniture for British manufacturers SCP and
Established & Sons among others, and was
the winner of the first Jerwood Furniture
Prize in 1999. His practice includes exhibition
design, installation work, curating and
writing on design. He has taught and lectured
in Britain and abroad, and is currently
Senior Tutor on the Design Products MA
at the Royal College of Art, London.
[British, born 1963]

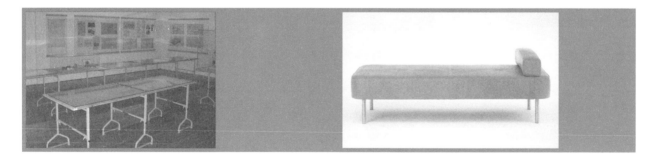

for thoughts on...

Are designers conflicted about priorities?

I remember at college a designer talking to us about his work. It was what I see as ridiculous curvy plastic stuff – executive desk sets, luxury goods with a capital L and a little bit of bling too. At the end of the talk he closed with an image of the world from outer space, saying that this is what really matters. It was gobsmackingly out of kilter with what he'd shown of his work, which was just expensive landfill. I thought it would have been better not to do some of that work than to show slides and talk about the bigger message.

What makes a design sustainable?

I hope that people don't only keep expensive things. I've got this cutlery from IKEA that cost about £25 and is beautifully simple and stainless steel – really lovely. I'm aware of it every day I use it. I'd like to think that as people live with and get used to this kind of thing, they grow to appreciate and love it regardless of its cost.

The craft is important to you...

The thing I like most is visiting a factory, seeing what happens and being able to interact with the process and work out how to use it most efficiently to get the job done. But sadly, furniture manufacturing is less and less about factories and more and more about the brand. I'm less interested in what drives a lot of modern commerce – so for me that fibreglass Eames chair you have over there is so great because it is so determined by understanding how it is made. This quality is part of what makes it sustainable too. The new ones are polyprop and recyclable. Fibreglass is nasty stuff to work with and you can't recycle it, but I don't think it matters so much when that's already lasted 40 years and will easily last another 40 or more. The new ones will need to be recycled, because they are so much less robust and will soon become grubby and rough-looking.

Glossary of ethical thought

→ 066
Buddhism

So, recycling isn't the only consideration?

In the '90s I remember going to the Design Museum for the launch of the watch derived from the Swiss railway clock. Recycling was getting lots of attention, so the man who headed the company said how the bodies were made out of recycled brass. I thought 'shut up, mate!'. Brass has always been recycled because it's got a scrap value, like all non-ferrous metals; that was the basis of the rag and bone trade. He belittled the value of the product by making too much of this stuff.

This is a complex argument. It's energy-inefficient to recycle sometimes, for example. It's very difficult to get a holistic sense of these things. There are life cycle analysis charts of materials and products, but they very rarely look at how this fits into the greater scheme of things. It's a bit like when the government pays a marketing company to prove how good nuclear power is over hydro or electric or solar power. You can make statistics support whatever you want.

Government should worry less about putting recycled logos on plastic bottles for example, and more about using less plastic in the first place. Packaging is absurd. There's such a stupid amount of plastic, cardboard, everything. Why don't we just look at what they do in Germany or Scandinavia? Why don't we just take a leaf out of their book? Speak to some Dutch people; they're not far away, so let's share some information.

How much do you consider these issues?

A lot. We're just talking about designing another exhibition for the Design Museum, and we're already thinking about reusing the glass from a previous exhibition. Exhibitions are often built to a very high spec, so there should be some kind of central depository for ex-exhibition fabric – whether it's the Chelsea Flower Show or the Ideal Home Show or some smaller thing at the Crafts Council. After one Crafts Council show I was involved in, they phoned round and asked whether anybody would be interested in the materials that they didn't need anymore – it could have been used in house building or certainly reused somehow.

What role does the media have?

The design media often gives attention to the wrong things. Take for example the new piece by Zaha Hadid for Established & Sons. It's a hugely excessive and expensive plastic table. It required a crane to get it in to the building when they showed it at the Milan furniture fair. It wouldn't go up the stairs or in the lift or through the doors. It turned out it wouldn't go through the hole in the roof, so they had to disassemble the roof.

It's the kind of thing you see in a Prada store with a couple of cashmere bikinis on it and it looks completely amazing. So that kind of makes it valid. But if you have to build the architecture around it, it's not really furniture design. It ignores the real requirements of furniture – being affordable, easy to produce and deliverable without a crane and a supersize truck. On one level it's interesting, it has an impact and it has a place in the world. A very small place, but that has to do with scales of production. But it can be dangerous because it gets so much press. This is particularly misleading for impressionable students.

Is its value in being groundbreaking?

Well, it's a step in another direction in terms of how furniture design evolves. There were square tables, then Charles Eames came along and took things in a slightly more organic direction. This is another step on that road – less plain, super curvaceous – the top's not flat, even. Kind of annoying when you want to put a glass of wine down, but…

Are artists respected more than designers?

I've recently done a couple of projects where I've had more the role of an artist. There were big empty gallery spaces that I had to fill, and it's been a nice experience. When you're a designer you're providing a service, not so different to being a plumber or whatever, but actually an artist is also providing a service. Commercial and public galleries are part of the entertainment industry now – you know the Barbican Gallery is competing with Leicester Square Odeon and Selfridges nowadays, isn't it?

That said, I did get more freedom and appreciation. The client was open-minded. I was commissioned because people were interested to see what I would do. So a free rein and support, as well as to try and achieve something that was discussed as an intellectual thing rather than a purely commercial thing.

for thoughts on...

→ 047
**Jacqueline Roach
on changing things
from within**

→ 102
Moral language

→ 128
**Simon Esterson
on capitalism**

→ 164–167
**The global and
business context
to design**

Is 'design' a misunderstood term?

Yes. The language is failing us a bit, isn't it? Don't eskimos have 11 words for cloud or rain? There should be 11 different words for design.

This is becoming more of a problem because marketing people have hijacked the term. Consumers aren't trained in design thinking, so they can't analyse for themselves whether something is a good buy or will be worn out by next year. They're almost trained to buy on the basis of superficial considerations – whatever colour or shape is deemed fashionable or marketed strongly. As a designer I gather things too, but not as a consumer, I'm not buying into someone's marketing thing. I still pull things out of skips or off the street because I'm interested in the form or how it's made or why it looks like it does.

This comes down to politics...

Capitalism is a bit berserk now, but it's a difficult one because we're all wrapped up in it. Unless you go and live in Wales in a tepee and grow your own vegetables, it's really difficult not to be a part of it. You have to live quite an extreme life to be removed from it, and you could argue that that's just avoiding doing something positive to change things. I think you can only make a difference from within. It's important to take part in the discussion.

Obviously the question is where you draw the line. There are issues for you as a graphic designer about representing the views of those you don't agree with, for example. Do you preach to the converted and work for a good cause, or work for more commercial enterprises and try to change things from within? Ultimately you need to feel comfortable with your own ethical position.

Glossary of ethical thought

→ **070, 071**
Marxism
Transcendentalism

Why are you involved in education?

I believe very strongly in it as a force for good. I know that's a big statement, but I think that it gives people the means and confidence to think for themselves. To learn to apply logic and rational thought, combined with empathy to understand the position of others. This dispels the idea that it is only religion that makes people behave well.

Design education helps you learn to analyse a situation or problem and initiate changes to make things better – if not solve the problem. You can apply this thinking to politics or anything else – not just design. I've often thought that there should be designers employed in government and at board level of big corporations to exercise that analytical process in solving problems. The solution isn't always another product. Often it's about thinking broadly and instigating systems to deal with a situation, which doesn't require more material being produced or processed.

It's great when you see students recognising these ideas. That makes it all very worthwhile. In an ideal world this would start at school. Years ago, the Design Council argued that design should be part of the national curriculum. I think it would equip people to deal with life much better if they had a broad understanding of what design might be.

Have you felt envious of other designers?

I did at one point for a couple of years. I was anxious that I should be more focused and more determined or ambitious or something and try and get more serious clients. I never really did anything about it, because I'm not very good at that. It was kind of niggling me that I was fannying about doing this and that, and not really focusing enough.

Then suddenly I realised I was really, really lucky to be in the position I'm in. I get to do lots of different things and I've worked with lots of different people and that's always been a really nice experience – working with other people who do other things, and just doing lots of different types of projects. Last year, for example, I did a few writing projects. I'm not a writer at all, but I'm a bit opinionated and so people think I might have something to say… and it was kind of interesting.

So are you actually quite happy?

Yeah, I am. I feel very lucky to get away with what I do and I enjoy it so much.

I think within my business I'm respected for what I do too, but that's not the thing that drives me, it's the fact that I'm happy. I think it gets more difficult to be happy, doesn't it? When I first left college my enthusiasm would override things that it wouldn't now. I'm still happy because I've got a variety of challenging work, so I'm learning. I've never aspired to having a holiday home or a flash car or anything. I think I'm lucky because little things make me happy.

You know the novelist Kurt Vonnegut? I heard him talking about how he writes on an old typewriter. He sends his manuscript to someone who types it up on a word processor. He buys one single envelope, walks to the post office, gets it weighed, buys the stamps and has a little chat with the person in the post office. He had a very nice way of talking about all that – the atmosphere of his life and how this is a contact with the world. It was a very nice kind of poetic thing and very warm and funny as well. I identify with that.

for thoughts on…

→ 037
**Anthony Grayling
on happiness**

→ 094–099
**Happiness and
quality of life**

→ 124
**Billie Tsien
on design education**

Paula Scher studied at the Tyler School of Art, Philadelphia, USA and was art director at both Atlantic and CBS Records before joining Pentagram New York as a partner. Scher's distinctive style incorporates an eclectic mix of historical design references and pop iconography. Her work includes identity, environmental graphics, packaging and publication design. She has received over 100 awards, including the Chrysler Award for Design Innovation and is a member of the Alliance Graphique Internationale. [American, born 1948]

I don't understand how the word 'good' is used here. Am I a well-behaved graphic designer? Am I a socially conscious graphic designer? Am I a designer who makes qualitative work (good, not excellent)? It's a rather peculiar question. Here's what I think I do: I design because I love to make things and get things made. I want the things that I make or get made to elevate the expectation of what design should be. That's what I try hard to do in every capacity. Sometimes, I even succeed in it. I can't determine whether or not that's 'good', I have to leave that to the critics and historians.

Children's Museum of Pittsburgh signage and wayfinding system
2005
Playfully exploiting the possibilities of language, scale and repetition, Scher's signage is fun, informative and specific to its young audience.

Oded Ezer graduated from the Bezalel Academy of Art and Design, Jerusalem and founded his studio Oded Ezer Typography in 2000 in Givatayim, Israel. Alongside his commercial design work, Ezer also runs experimental typo-art projects exploring Hebrew typography. These works have been published worldwide, and have won numerous international awards. Ezer was co-founder of the first cooperative of Israeli font designers, Ha'Gilda (The Guild) and is a member of the ICD (Israel Community of Designers). [Israeli, born 1972]

Between 'problem solving' and 'free expression', I prefer to describe design as the field that acts between need and fantasy. 'Good design' according to this approach, is design that can answer both things successfully. My own motivation to create is to challenge the borders of typographic conventions and to suggest alternative solutions. Some of the questions I often ask myself while creating are: 'How does typography "behave" in different situations?'; 'How will typographic design look 100 years from now?'; 'How can one use the tension between literal meaning and visual meaning in typographic work?'. I see myself as someone who uses his abilities to change and reshape the visual appearance of our environment in a way that will reflect reality, instead of hiding it. I see this as not only a visual or professional act, but also a political one. So... am I a good designer?

The Message
2001
A self-published typographic homage to the music of the Israeli composer Arye Shapira. Exploring how letters would behave if they were music, this poster communicates an emotional rather than conventionally readable message.

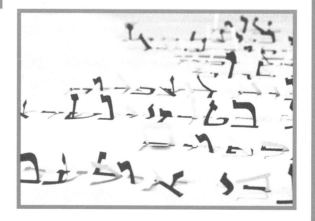

Divya Chadha studied fine art at the University of Delhi, India. After graduation, Chadha worked as a graphic designer in advertising and communication agencies in New Delhi, where she was involved in brand building and brand management. She has worked as a freelance designer in the areas of web design and corporate identity, and is currently studying for her MA in Graphic Design at London College of Communication, England. [Indian, born 1982]

I wonder if you mean 'good at what I do' or 'good by virtue of what I do'? It's possible to say that both are related, at least in my view. Interestingly, it has been suggested by the philosopher Vilém Flusser that the designer 'is a cunning plotter laying his traps'. I don't know if being a good designer would mean I'd take a stand against designing a campaign for a cigarette brand, innovate and create an award-winning and original design concept, provide the most effective and economic solution to my client's problem or design for the underprivileged. In my opinion, being good is not as easy as that. I think I am a good designer because I realise I am responsible for the messages that are being sent out through the visual communication that I have designed. I am responsible for the form and content of the design that is aimed at an audience or consumer, its quality and effect – be it good or bad.

Painted signage of New Delhi
2006
A photo of a painted sign in New Delhi from Chadha's MA project, which examines the role of vernacular hand-rendered signage in the visual culture of the city and explores its reason and function.

Billie Tsien studied fine arts at Yale before gaining her Masters in Architecture from the University of California, USA. With partner Tod Williams she founded Tod Williams Billie Tsien Architects (TWBTA), an architectural practice that crosses disciplinary boundaries and creates lyrical buildings bridging the worlds of architecture and fine arts. Tsien and Williams seek to bring out the humanity of buildings, whether private residences or public institutions, and their award-winning projects include the Neurosciences Institute in La Jolla, California and the American Folk Art Museum in New York City, which received the Arup World Architecture Award for Best Building in the World. Tsien is on the board of the Public Art Fund, the American Academy in Rome and the Architectural League.
[American, born 1949]

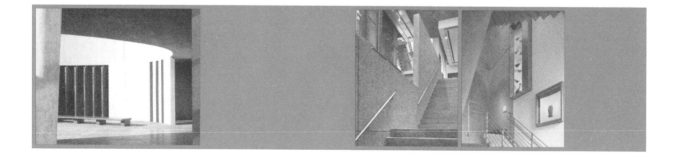

for thoughts on...

→ 055
**Richard Holloway
on humility**

→ 148
**Billie Tsien/
examples**

Philosophy

We see architecture as an act of profound optimism. Its foundation lies in believing that it is possible to make places on the earth that can give a sense of grace to life – and believing that that matters. It is what we have to give and it is what we leave behind.

We wrote these words a number of years ago and believe in them even more deeply today. We measure the value of our work by the quiet pleasure of the lives lived in our buildings. We want to solve problems and we want to transcend solutions. We try to work with a thoughtful integrity to make buildings that will last and be loved. We want to leave good marks upon this earth.

This work comes from two voices and from many voices.

© 2006
Tod Williams Billie Tsien Architects

How important is longevity to your work?

Everything is transient. We feel great joy in making something that lasts longer than we do, but with this comes a huge responsibility. I tell students that most people don't have the opportunity to be involved in something that extends beyond their lives and that this is a great gift. So, this desire to make something that lasts is determined partly by the knowledge that as human beings we are not lasting.

Because of this awareness it's very important to us that a building is executed beautifully. This isn't necessarily a prevailing criterion in architecture. I am not judgemental about this. For me though, it is important to care about what we are doing. I don't want to be responsible for something that is only made to last for a few years. This is one of the reasons why we have avoided more commercial work. A restaurant is unlikely to be around for ten years but a library, one hopes, will be around for 50.

This seems quite humble...

Our job is to be useful, but we also aspire to transcend that, and in doing so that's not very humble. We're interviewing for a project with a church at the moment and have had some interesting discussions as a result. The clients have talked about vertical Christians and horizontal Christians. Vertical Christians are focused on the cross, horizontal Christians are much more interested in the community. So, I would say that in terms of humility we're pretty horizontal, but we have some vertical also.

Is it distressing to see demolished buildings?

If it's a good building then yes, this is distressing. If it's a building that's not being used or there is potential for something better, then I don't feel upset. I think use is very important. Buildings are not monuments in and of themselves. Use has to be attached to them. Architecture is art and use in a balance.

What do you mean by 'quiet pleasure'?

Basically I am quite a shy person and I feel more comfortable sitting in the corner reading a book. I appreciate places where one can have some sense of reflection. It's not that we're always trying to make places a sanctuary, but rather than mirror chaos we probably look to mirror quiet and then let someone else come in and make the chaos. We are probably more directed to making a container that is quiet so that it can hold other people's noise.

Glossary of ethical thought

→ 066
Buddhism
Confucianism

Does this relate to happiness?

This makes me think of our son. I have learnt so much watching him growing up. When you are with a small child, happiness is so direct. As an adult you are often in a hurry, you have your goals, you are focused on getting things done – but a kid will stop in their tracks. So, he would see a berry on a bush and get so excited – there would be a huge burst of pleasure. That ability to take pleasure in smallness is something that we are very interested in exploring in our work. There are details enfolded in our work that you discover, or don't discover. I think our buildings have a gravity to them, but they also have an optimism.

Is yours an optimistic profession?

Most people who become architects do so in the face of a lot of obstacles. I suppose being an architect has more credibility than saying that you are a modern dancer or a poet, but it's still a profession where you are bucking the odds because it is still hard to make something nice. So, you will only do that, and struggle to keep on doing it, because you believe it makes a difference to people's lives. If you believe you can make a difference that is essentially optimistic.

Is it hard to keep true to these beliefs?

It is difficult. You are dealing with a lot of people – inside your studio, outside your studio and the client of course. You are connecting with them all and trying to draw them together to make a beautiful bow. It can be very frustrating but it only takes the words of one person when you're done, who says something wonderful or positive about the place that you have made and it's hugely gratifying. That can balance 100 days of frustration.

What are some of your frustrations?

It took me about ten years to really decide to carry on as an architect. I felt for a long time that I was spending too much time doing this and that instead of doing what I wanted, which was more drawing – I didn't feel very creative. But I came to realise that all aspects of the work are creative. This isn't always convincing, but I try to remember it. A lot of what I do now is writing letters and so on, but it is all part of the act of being creative. Being creative is not all about sitting on your own and making something.

Is compromise necessary?

Sometimes compromise is good, sometimes you fight against it, but sometimes you also need to join hands and learn from other people. As a young architect you think you have to be extremely hard-nosed and control in a masterful way. One of the things that you understand as you grow older is that if you can make an alliance or partnership with a client, and not be false in that, then you too can learn. This sounds very new age, but it is worth trying to find something in people that you can embrace.

Do you see teaching as sharing?

We teach every couple of years and get a huge amount from it. The students bring their own personalities, their energy and interest in other things that we perhaps haven't paid attention to. We also end up going to lectures, which we never do when we are studio-based. I think what we bring to the students is different to those people who teach all the time. We're perhaps not as good teachers, but we're probably good life coaches. We talk about how we work and how we get things done. Although we give them crits on their design, I think most of our value is that we are very grounded.

Do you discuss your ethics with students?

I don't know that I would feel comfortable designing something like a prison and as I don't feel comfortable with our government there are aspects of government jobs that I would not be interested in doing. I would also be wary of some developers, but I think students are in a different place right now.

Students are interested in working for developers because with it comes power and money. I feel strangely from another time. I make essentially moral judgements, but students think of jobs as opportunities. I do find this distressing. Things always swing back and forth but at the moment quite young people seem fairly conservative. I have always associated youth with being the opposite, so this is surprising to me.

Yours seems an ethical approach...

I guess our approach is an ethical one. This is manifested in the buildings themselves and our approach to others. We try to treat people well in our studio and those we work with in all other ways. This is about respecting other people – a simple word, but actually very hard to do. In the making of our buildings we try to respect the place and respect the potential of the future. So this is the way we operate. It is always a struggle to be true to that, but that's about being alive. Struggle is good even though it's not easy.

for thoughts on...

→ 094–099
Happiness and quality of life

→ 118
Michael Marriott on design education

Will Holder studied at the Academy of Art and Design, 's-Hertogenbosch, The Netherlands before moving to Amsterdam where he is an independent graphic designer. A guiding principle in Holder's work is evolving forms of language as a means of public address, and his varied practice includes commissions for dotdotdot magazine and the Tourette's II evenings he organises in Amsterdam Art Gallery W139. He is currently translating William Morris's News from Nowhere (An Epoch of Rest) as a guide for design education and practice. [British, born 1969]

Postal stamps
2005
A set of ten stamps, commissioned by the TPG (Dutch Post Office) to commemorate the fiftieth anniversary of the World Press Photo foundation. Almost every year's winning photo depicts war or political violence.

Love thy Neighbour
Find and replace 'friendship' with 'design':

I think I have learned the most about myself through friendships, and found such friends in people I have never known, or are long dead. Friendships are formed with people you can listen to forever, not minding if they repeat themselves. Friends can make you truly laugh and truly make you cry. Friends are not embarrassed when they see you naked. In friendships it is not a problem to say nothing, and you will not butt in when a friend is talking, there is time enough to state your own opinion. Friends are people you can share a thousand words with, by using two. It is not necessary to agree with a friend, but to understand the nature of the disagreement. You don't choose your parents; you do choose your friends. Friendships can last forever.

This text has two precursors: News from Nowhere by William Morris, a tale of a future society where everyone calls each other 'neighbour' and the production of (freely exchanged) goods and services is preceded by a simple concept of equality. The second is from Heidegger, who described books as merely voluminous letters written to (future) friends.

Simon Esterson is a self-taught designer. He started his career at the Architects' Journal before co-founding Blueprint magazine, where his rational approach to design and layout won wide acclaim. Renowned for his editorial design, Esterson has shaped the look of many journals and magazines, including the Guardian newspaper, where he was consulting art director, and the international architectural magazine Domus, where he was creative director. He redesigned the film magazine Sight and Sound, and has consulted on The Times, the Observer and the Sunday Telegraph newspapers. His book and catalogue designs include publications for the Royal Academy of Arts, the Hayward Gallery and Tate Publishing. Esterson is director of Esterson Associates and is a Royal Designer for Industry. [British, born 1958]

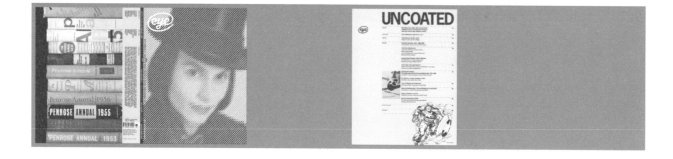

for thoughts on...

Is your work less commercial than some?

I really just do editorial work – newspapers, books, magazines – a little separate world outside the mainstream of graphic design. Obviously the reader is paying towards the publication, but with newspapers and magazines the majority of the revenue comes through advertising sales. If you don't have enough readers you can't trigger the right advertising – a national brand won't advertise if the circulation is less than a few hundred thousand copies. The advertiser buys space and there are legal and ethical requirements about what goes in it, which is nothing to do with me. The idea that advertisers could influence editorial is clearly wrong, and so there are many people watching for this – publishers and editors and so on. But most magazines wouldn't exist without this revenue, so I can't claim that my work isn't commercial, it's absolutely commercial.

Are there political implications?

I tend not to work for the Guardian's competitors because you are compromised if you compete with something that you are involved in. Fortunately the Guardian is the paper I read, so there isn't a dilemma there.

Are any types of work more 'ethical'?

The simplistic view is that any public sector or arts organisation is okay, as are charities, but anything corporate is terrible. But organisations that rely on public revenue are funded largely from taxes that are levied on corporate activity. Many of these bodies have corporate sponsors too, and even personal donations to charities are not necessarily 'clean'.

Let's suppose you only work for government departments – but every two years they spend valuable resources on redesigning their corporate identities. Then when it comes to being treated decently, I've had just as much trouble with arts bodies as any corporate client.

Is behaving well compromising?

We all know people who do fantastic work, but are terrible business people or absolute shits. The kind of drive that gets your idea through is the same drive that makes you difficult to work with. You cannot disconnect the politics and aesthetics of somebody's work and the politics of the way they do their business, can you? But, for most designers somebody's rocky reputation isn't relevant when set against a stunning piece of work – it's this that will live on.

Glossary of ethical thought

→ 066
Confucianism

Do we have the choice to be ethical?

A great deal is predetermined by the system you live under – in our case capitalism. What does a client do, faced with a quote from printer A, who uses recycled paper and waterless or alcohol-free printing processes, but is ten per cent more expensive? Then there's printer B, based in Britain, but a print broker. You get value for money but have no knowledge of who the printer actually is, and therefore no idea about processes used or labour conditions. Then what about printer C, in China and cheaper than A and B? It's a developing economy, but you know nothing about the environmental circumstances or the labour relations. The repercussions? One is that the British print industry will cease to exist… and that's just the placing of one print job.

Should we consider access in our work?

Guidelines exist, and designers should be aware of them. There needs to be balance though. This is a grey area and good work can be rejected unnecessarily as a result. When I was working at the Guardian, we put the chess puzzle in colour in one of the sections. We had a letter from a reader who was colour-blind and couldn't do it anymore. The next day it was changed of course.

Do we need solidarity with other designers?

Let's take free pitching. We don't do it. Ideally nobody would, but that's each designer's ethical choice. I think that a potential client should at least make a contribution towards costs. It makes it a more serious enterprise for them, which is in everyone's best interests. The ideal is for paid competitive pitches involving only three or four designers.

Should we be producing less?

I think this is happening with newspapers and magazines, but more for a capital market-driven reason than for an ethical one. With increasing online information, the market for these products shrinks and becomes more specialised. It's concentrated on people who value reading as circulation declines and advertising disappears to the web. The comparison now would be between the Sun, which is cheap, has a lot of advertising in it and is a mass-market product, and the London Review of Books, which has very little advertising and a high cover price, but you're clearly paying for its intellectual energy and rigour.

Do we create desire that can't be satisfied?

I suppose we have to recognise that unsated desire keeps us all employed, so we are understandably protective of our skills in fashion and ideas – even if we don't produce it in the West, we can think it. Constant buying drives the economy, which potentially brings prosperity for all. It's odd that because of global warming we are telling Africa, India and China that they can't have what we have. It's an imperialist attitude. I'm not saying that the solution to Africa's problems is more branding of course. Undoubtedly there is a danger of a visual and design overload – just occasionally I think maybe we could just stop here and concentrate on something or somebody else.

How do you think of money in our business?

My mother was a teacher and she was appalled when my second job on Fleet Street yielded more than hers – we were both quite disgusted in a way.

I think the more you get paid as a designer, the less control you have over the job. That's my broad theory. It's not always true – you can get involved with a worthy, low budget organisation who will still interfere, but then you have the choice to go ahead, but absent yourself from the design process – or to walk away. If you are paid lots of money it's difficult to do that. Money is a fantastic corrupter of aesthetic ideals.

Beauty and ethics aren't mutually exclusive…

No, although beauty is subjective and very much about context. In this respect I admire Adolf Loos's ideas about function and truth that say 'this door handle might not be in the Museum of Modern Art, but when you put your hand on it it's quite nice and it opens the door well'.

It is possible for graphic design to delight and enrich people's experience and to still work. Fashion and zeitgeist can cloud our ability to discriminate of course – something is wonderful one minute and passé the next – and if the focus is making 'special' graphic design, then the value of function is demoted. That's when you get designers saying to their clients, 'I know you wanted a leaflet, but I thought it much more fun if I took all your money and made a very big pink wall. I think there just aren't enough pink walls in the world'.

I got depressed in that period when graphic designers justified illegible, visually experimental typography by saying, 'it doesn't matter, the copy's rubbish'. If it is rubbish, don't produce it. I like to think that this doesn't apply to the projects I work on. Editorial clients want people to read what they produce.

Can work distract us from existential angst?
All creative activity can.

Do clients know it's so personally important?
No. We're usually making an object
for somebody, but wanting it to be our object too.
Of course there's the client's brief and the end-user,
but there's your designer ego too and I think you
have to be a very, very good designer to be free of it.

Does your work make you happy?
Sometimes it does, but if asked
'What's your favourite project?' it would be the next
one. You live in hope that your next project will
have everything. I suppose this is about wanting
work to be perfect in the terms that you have
set up for it. But I think you have to be slightly
suspicious of the pursuit of perfection. The world
is this kind of shitty, mixed up place. I think that's
something about getting older, you realise nothing's
perfect and it's actually fine to go with the flow.
The most wonderful meal is at its most wonderful
the moment it's in front of you, before you eat
anything. As the meal goes on you're enjoying it –
but more in your mind, in the ordering and maybe
the preparation, and certainly the delivery of it. As
you eat it you get a bit full, and a bit fed up, and you
realise that everything is just transient really.
Perfection is relative of course. If you
design annual reports using eight colours and
two spot varnishes, then newspapers seem poorly
printed. But if you work on newspapers and see the
Guardian, the print quality seems beautiful. Object
quality is what's important, in the broadest sense, so
an example is a fantastically realised newspaper –
a useful and attractive object. You have to consider
the content. For me this often makes
the annual report imperfect, if not unpleasant.
Something that makes me unhappy
is a waste of time, hope and energy. There's nothing
worse than a job that sets off in one direction
and then somebody who hasn't been involved
before changes it.

Is graphic design important?
Above a certain Plimsoll line of
survivability it becomes special, enriching,
engaging and can be fun. Below that line, it's one
of the things that could go really, isn't it? Even
information design; everybody can get a bit of chalk
and mark an arrow on a wall – mammoths this way,
tigers that way, you know.

Glossary of ethical thought

→ 067
Aristotelianism

→ 072
Existentialism

Being good   **Simon Esterson**   128 : 129

thomas.matthews are Sophie Thomas and Kristine Matthews. They met as students at the Royal College of Art, London, UK and formed their communication design agency on graduating. Grounded in graphic design, their practice encompasses print and web design, exhibition design and wayfinding systems for clients including the Imperial War Museum, Action Aid and The Architecture Foundation. thomas.matthews creates interactive project solutions and focuses on including the audience. Consideration of the environmental impact of design is integral to its work.
[British, born 1973/American, born 1969]

What is a good designer? A good designer knows the correct kerning for Bell Gothic. But we hope it goes a bit deeper than that. A good designer can also get inspiration from anything: a peeling wall, a foreign bus ticket, a mistake. But is that 'good' enough? So much of what designers produce is wasteful. Do we really need those 10,000 new leaflets, any more than we really need the snazzy new product that they're advertising? A good designer creates communication that is inspiring, meaningful and sustainable. That means questioning. Questioning the brief, questioning the way things get done. Setting parameters and challenges even when the client doesn't demand it. Printing on post-consumer papers with vegetable-based inks. Avoiding PVC. Designing for double duty – if you need to design a leaflet and an envelope, can it not be the same thing? Sourcing locally so that goods don't need to travel so far. Cranking the creative process up a notch to get really interesting and original solutions. Good designers love a challenge: making something that's not just beautiful, but smart too. It's good fun.

The British Council Pavilion at Glastonbury
2005
A flexible, reusable space constructed from locally coppiced birch and a changeable internal printed canvas skin. At night the structure is lit from within, creating an illuminated lantern effect.

James Victore **is a self-taught graphic designer who lives in – and loves – New York. His provocative and strikingly bold imagery has won awards from most of the major national and international design competitions, including an Emmy award for television animation. His clients have included Amnesty International, the Portfolio Centre and Moët & Chandon. Victore teaches at the School of Visual Arts in New York City and is a former member of the Alliance Graphique Internationale.** [American, born 1962]

The present political situation in America and the subsequent reaction (or lack thereof) from designers makes us all afraid – afraid of losing and afraid of not having enough. We know Bush is wrong, but we hope he is right. Plus, it is very expensive to get any message out these days. It's expensive to have an opinion. Most of the stuff I see is crappy graphic design-driven vector art, not real human emotion driven by need. Humans make statements, not designers. Designers decorate. Any 'good' work I have done comes from a real need to make an honest statement to real humans. It was not driven by the feeble hope to get into the pages of Print magazine.

Bush Pirate
2002
A poster commissioned by the American Institute of Graphic Arts, New York City and reprinted by Victore at studio expense for the group International ANSWER, Act Now to Stop War and End Racism.

Chris de Bode started travelling and taking photographs after leaving school and began his photographic career while working as a professional mountain climbing instructor. Now a freelance photojournalist based in Amsterdam, de Bode's first work was for commercial and editorial clients in Holland, before travelling to the Middle East where he documented both sides of the conflict between the Israelis and the Palestinians. His widely published work ranges from portraits of earthquake victims in El Salvador and casualties of war in northern Uganda to reportage of the construction and consequences of the Three Gorges Dam on the Yangtze River, China. He is currently completing a project on cycle races across the world that includes reportage of the tours of Colombia, Senegal, Eritrea and Qatar.
[Dutch, born 1965]

for thoughts on...

→ **017–032**
Freedom and responsibility in the arts

→ **038, 039**
Anthony Grayling on beauty and ethics

→ **154**
Chris de Bode/ examples

Are photojournalism and ethics connected?

Yes. Taking pictures is subjective in that you can direct the viewer in a very specific way, so you have to be careful about telling the truth. I can't change the world, but I try to show what is happening in a direct way. I try to make pictures that people can easily relate to. I believe in seducing people with a beautiful image and then getting the message across. That's the way I photograph and that's the way I edit in the end. In that sense I am pretty present in my pictures. My hand is there. People are struck by the directness of my way of communicating so in some sense I succeed in transmitting the message.

Can you ensure you are telling a truth?

I hardly ever take pictures of subjects I know nothing about. I gather information and talk with people so that I can make the right decisions in showing the subject. But I don't hesitate, for example when I take a portrait, to intervene – to ask people to move to the left or right, or to perform an action. In reportage it's very different, things just happen as they do.

I'm very hesitant about directing the opinion of the viewer. For example, if I'm asked to photograph a demonstration of Moroccan youth here in Amsterdam, and to show them negatively, I won't orchestrate it – that's not right. You can't stigmatise people because the media would like you to. I was asked to do a story about the murder of Theo van Gogh. I went with a journalist who spoke to various people asking if they knew the murderer – his family, his mother – he asked people who were Moroccan, but were not involved with the murder. I refused to take street pictures of them. It would stigmatise them. Instead, I went to the murderer's house and photographed the washing line with its wooden pegs to show that he was also doing his laundry just like you and me.

What's your attitude to image manipulation?

I believe I am allowed to change pictures in the way I would have done in a darkroom using chemicals. So, I can clean them and change the contrast. I will make things darker and lighter so the viewer's attention is attracted to the lighter spots – in that sense I manipulate the viewer. I try to make the subject in my picture as strong as possible. I work quite a bit within these limits because I think it can make pictures stronger and more dramatic.

Is photojournalism always political?

It's very rare to see photographs that are really unbiased and give freedom to draw different conclusions. Once a photographer is working on a story that sets out to explore a problem there is an agenda. Most of the time photojournalism is political in that it reveals the photographer's private opinion, but transmitting a very strong political view is quite rare.

Are there publications you wouldn't work for?

It depends how publications use my pictures – if it's out of context I feel very upset. It doesn't happen often. I've got my favourite newspapers, of course, and if I have a new series of pictures I will contact them and not the ones that I'm unsympathetic to. In many cases the pictures are sold through agencies, but they are pretty careful about the usage of pictures. Broadly, I want everybody to be able to show my pictures. I believe that I am only the messenger and the more people that look at my message, the better. So, I don't have a strong opinion about which publications reproduce my work.

Do you feel compromised by clients?

Nowadays people contact me because they have seen my photos and they like what I'm doing, so they give me a free hand. We talk about things and I am briefed in a way, but I think it's my way of looking at the world that people want to publish.

Time is a constraint. I am pretty well trained to find metaphors for different subjects, so if I can't succeed in finding the real story or the real event I make a strong metaphor, which expresses that problem. So, time-wise and money-wise I have to compromise, but I think that's part of the challenge – finding the pieces of the puzzle that convey the full story.

Who do you feel most responsible to?

The subject of the picture.

Do you worry about upsetting the viewer?

I don't mind if people feel uncomfortable or worried when they look at a picture, but I don't see the need to show excessive violence or things that are disrespectful to the people within the picture.

Are you ever in danger?

Not often, because I normally work with NGOs and so have contacts on the ground before I go somewhere. I always make sure that the moment I arrive there is someone to look after me. It can be a driver or local staff of an NGO – people who know more about the place than I do. That makes me feel comfortable, as soon as that is arranged I feel very free to walk around and do my work. I wouldn't go to cities that are under fire. I wouldn't mind going to northern Iraq, but I wouldn't go to real danger zones.

I like working with NGOs. It works with my personal situation too. I've got a family, I can't be away from home for too long. I can go for a week, a week and a half, two weeks, but never for a month or so and all NGO assignments are pretty short.

Is it a distressing occupation?

Yes, and it's lonely. I've got my little book with me in my hotel room – I make notes to release tension. I experience situations that are so sad. In a way I've learned to be more empathetic than sympathetic, because I have to protect myself. I work sometimes with Doctors Without Borders, and their professional attitude helps me in dealing with some tragic situations. But I don't want to become so professional that things become normal that are not normal at all. So you have to be alert to your inner self. I try never to be ignorant of a situation or say 'shit happens, this is Africa, whatever'. I try to be as sensitive as I can within certain limitations, or else I can't function anymore.

Do you self-fund personal projects?

Yes. Right now I'm working on a book about cycling races in third world countries. I fund it through other publications. It's my thing and a boy's dream to do it. I explore socio-economics or political situations through sports. It's quite hard financially to produce self-initiated projects. I don't look for subsidies or grants – I always try to do it on my own. But within these restrictions I love doing it. It gives me freedom as I always try to find subjects that are really close to my heart. This book will be finished early next year and then I'll try to find something new. That's how it all started in a way, pursuing some dreams and approaching them with positive energy.

for thoughts on...

→ 049
**Jacqueline Roach
on professionalism**

→ 110
**Designers as citizens
of the world**

→ 189
**Dan Eatock
on self-initiated projects**

**Deborah Szebeko both
trained and worked in advertising before
becoming disillusioned. She chose
to study for an MA at London College of
Communication, UK and became a project
manager at Great Ormond Street Children's
Hospital. Motivated by her experiences
as a designer within the healthcare
environment, Szebeko started thinkpublic,
a health-focused service design and
communications agency, of which she is
director. thinkpublic works in collaboration
with patients and frontline staff
to empower user-groups to lead the
process of service design.
[British, born 1980]**

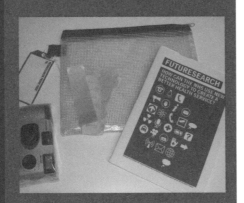

Futuresearch
2005
thinkpublic co-creates feedback
systems that involve listening
and learning from patients
and staff. These use graphic
tools to facilitate discussions
in which users are encouraged
to express and communicate
their views. Futuresearch was
conducted by thinkpublic for
the Spaceworks research centre
at King's College London.

**The imperative for 'good' designers is
to start by asking, 'What is the value of
this piece of design?'. Is it adding noise to
people's lives, or is it helping someone
in some way? We must question what value
our work adds to our personal growth as
designers, and challenge what messages
we are currently portraying to the public
about the design industry and how
we apply our skills. What is the value of
designing disposable noise, when there
are so many real-life challenges in the public
sector awaiting some TLC? Yet it's not
just about changing focus from the private
to public sector; the role of the 'good'
designer is evolving and entering exciting
new territory. We can use our skills to
empower people and give them a voice,
supporting individuals and communities
to co-design and articulate their ideas
and experiences into user-led policies,
services, communications and products.
Co-creating designs that are not only
produced in consultation with the user,
but are created and led by them, provides
a new experience and understanding
of design – and of the public sector. It
encourages the state to improve services,
and leads to design solutions that really
benefit and meet the needs of the public.**

Sheila Levrant de Bretteville
is Professor and Director of Studies in
Graphic Design at Yale University, USA.
She studied art history at Barnard College,
Columbia University and received her
MFA in graphic design from Yale. Her work
as a graphic designer, educator and public
artist stimulates awareness of the people,
subjects and voices that dominant culture
often fails to accommodate or celebrate, and
reflects her belief in the importance of user
participation in design. Her public artworks
and graphic design are widely published,
and her work is represented in collections
and exhibitions. De Bretteville established
the first women's design programme at the
California Institute for the Arts in 1971
and founded the Woman's Graphic Centre
at the Woman's Building in Los Angeles.
[American, born 1940]

for thoughts on...

Politics and ethics impact on your work...

For me politics and ethics are more about '...' than '!!!'. Considering all others as equals is both a political and ethical concern. My thoughts move toward ways of making that provide models for inclusion – who and what has been overlooked and devalued, and how I can bring those at the periphery into public view. This concern, and wanting to keep ambiguities and contradictions intact, has been a defining factor in my work as a designer, artist and educator. Every year I shudder during the admissions process even, as we make those kinds of discerning and exclusionary decisions! I think it important not to make overstatements about what we as designers do.

Is humility important in your work?

Yes! I find the hubris of the US abroad and at home odious and totally lacking in humility! In opposition, if for no other reason, I want my work to be expressive of humility – a contribution in its own modest way.

Can graphic designers contribute socially?

Designers have to make their own choices as to how best to contribute to our shared culture. All graphic design is by its nature social, so it is a matter of which kinds of social engagements are most desirable to you.

I tend to make choices on the basis of who I want to spend time with, as much as the type of project it is. I want to support those working for social change, but the people who work from a moral high ground are not necessarily the people with whom I want to work. I would rather donate to social causes and then pour my creative energy into projects that provide what is not already in place, where the people most need what it is I do best.

An objective for designers is to find clients who want what it is you want to do. It's a more equal exchange that way. That is what our students try to do, by creating a body of work that clearly has a coherent visual method and then looking for clients whose content is most open to the way they as designers want to work.

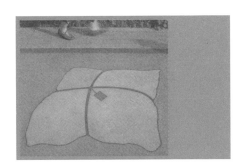

You often work with local communities...

Yes. I do not trust large organisations, and generally try to stay below the radar of the power structures in which I live and work, making my contribution as directly as possible to the community in which I am working. This is equally true whether it is a donation to a pastor in a church in New Orleans after the flood rather than to the American Red Cross, or in my site-specific work or in teaching.

At a site or even at Yale I like to first just 'hang out' in the community where I will be doing my work, getting a sense of what and who is there, and trying to find out what could enhance opportunities to hear and see one another better. It is always a negotiation, but less with who is paying me. It is more with those who are there now, as we weave their narratives with those who were there before them. Now that I have done this with many people – Japanese Americans in Los Angeles, African Americans in New Haven and a very eclectic mix of the working poor in Boston and Rhode Island – I have found some themes that recur in neighbourhoods with immigrant populations. I find I have an affinity with these kinds of issues and connections even though I am a white, middle-aged, middle-class woman, albeit the daughter of Jewish Polish immigrants.

Are designers sometimes self-obsessed?

Perhaps we ought to consider being selfish as underrated, and misunderstood. Without a sense of self it is much harder to be honest about why we do what we do. A healthy self-interest is just the kind of focus a graduate student needs to sustain an intense interest and commitment to the development of their work. They are taking the time to find out what they do best, and to enhance and enrich that inclination and skill with the extraordinary resources here at Yale. Our whole graduate graphic design programme has been developed to enable our students to take advantage of the entire university. My colleague Lisa Strausfeld called this being 'media agnostic' because our students respond to the ideas that we present to them in whichever medium they choose – print, motion, interactive, environmental – from their own perspective and with the visual method they develop here. The more focused and flexible that visual method, and iterative the process, the more centred that designer has become. This is selfishness and self-absorption in the best sense, as it enables egalitarian collaboration.

Can we devise ethical codes of practice?

Perhaps we first need to recognise that ethical dilemmas are in everything we do, and be tolerant because we all make mistakes. As a parent you have to believe you get more than one chance to say the right thing. Every day is a new day in which to say that which will best guide your child. The objective is to enable them to think for themselves to do the right thing in whichever society they find themselves. This is the goal not only for a parent or teacher, but for the viewer of work too. We're talking here about small and thoughtful choices, small devices. It is important to remember that ethical considerations aren't clear-cut and are often contingent inventions! I use question marks or ellipses in my work to imply this lack, that everything is not resolved, not everyone is included here and thus to make a place for absence with the '...'.

I find it best not to assume anything about anyone else, but move toward them positively with unconditional acceptance. This tends to help reveal the problems and concerns that they have. I have found in my work and teaching that having a genuine interest in how the other person thinks and sees the situation helps dissolve us/them oppositions. Looking at yourself from how the other sees you is hard to do, so instead ask what the other person sees. It is always better to ask and listen intently. Rather than big declarative statements (!!!) I consider situations more anecdotally, specifically and contingently.

What practical example might there be?

A starting point in developing an ethical code of graphic design practice could be to look at areas considered by other professions. In print graphics let's look at the way costs are hidden as perks of the job as an example. This would include mark-ups on print. Many designers carry the printing costs and add a percentage on top, but don't tell the client. For me this is an act of deception. It was first suggested to me by a printer who said all the designers she worked with in Los Angeles did it. I prefer to be transparent with my clients, so either I tell them this is the case or I don't do it.

I understand designers justify doing this by saying that they don't feel able to charge adequately for their time. Regardless of this, I just couldn't do it. It has to do with how I feel. I do not intend here to extrapolate big moral issues from small actions. It has to do with what makes me feel coherent. I suppose I want to conduct myself according to principles I learned from my parents about how to be honest in the world and leave it a better place in some way. It's not about judging others because I know that we all negotiate with ourselves about what is right and wrong, and in so doing justify all sorts of behaviour. This is all about the story we each tell ourselves, explaining what we are doing and why.

What about respect for others?

Which others? If we think of respecting the people who see the work as the client, how does the work change? It has become increasingly important to me to devise ways of welcoming the viewer into the creation of meaning in my work. I started inserting ambiguity and various meanings and voices, some more obvious and others less so, and then later leaving '…'.

Let's also consider how we think about the clients who pay us for the work. Clients have knowledge, just as designers do. Sharing this is a respectful exchange. This is about equality and engagement. This is true of teacher/student, client/designer and people-in-the-neighbourhood/ designer relationships.

Students see a life of constraints and limitations behind and in front of them, and want new ways to work that respect them and their way of working. For the two years that my students are here, my colleagues and myself carry these young designers in our minds so that when we see something that would interest them we share it with them. We each try to understand what they want to do and help them do it. They are our clients.

Glossary of ethical thought

→ 071
**Kierkegaard
Nietzsche**

→ 073
Virtue ethics

Being good   Sheila Levrant de Bretteville   138 : 139

Are there clients we shouldn't work for?

The number of areas that designers would really choose not to work in are very limited; some would design ads for cigarettes, and others would not. I use graphic design to say that it is not in my name that America has gone to war with Iraq, others would not. We make these choices finally because of who we are and how we want to be in the world.

From a teaching point of view, I try to be very careful about positions of moral superiority and do not assume I know what others think or are aligned with. There is a kind of hubris that comes with thinking that what you make is 'for the social good' and on a higher moral plane than other graphic design work. I recoil from that kind of self-importance and exceptionally prideful display of goody-goodiness. For instance, when I saw students who had made pro-choice T-shirts denigrate those who would not buy or wear them, I was troubled. I saw that they had no interest in conversing with those students whose position was also an ethical one, but who had come to a different conclusion. Additionally, those people with the minority view felt left out. One person's content is not better than another in an educational context where open discussion of divergent views on a subject is part of the agreement – we are here to learn from one another.

There's an argument that graphic design engenders desires for things to own and ways to look that can never be attained or satisfied, and that this is unethical. I don't quite go along with this as it denies the will of the person who sees the work. Although sometimes these images and texts promote something unhealthy or unsafe, I am not the moral arbiter of these choices. Viewers make their own choices of what they want to do and look like.

Is it necessary to be happy in your work?

Happiness, like comfort, is overrated. Both can breed insensitivity to those without the access, ability, possibility and privilege to have either. Whose happiness is more important, mine or someone else's? What makes me happy may make another person unhappy and that in turn may make me unhappy. That is why contradictions and ambiguities are welcome in my work, in teaching, and in the admissions process. The discomfort anyone feels about a work or action can be enhancing to that person and to a community.

Is there a relationship of beauty to ethics?

Even if only for a moment, if a work of design can be transcendent for someone else as well as the maker, it is not only worth doing, but also is in a sense beautiful. I have noticed that the b word has been more or less acceptable at different times, but traditionally it is the subject of philosophical debate. I am inclined to diffuse and decentralise the ideal, as each person's beauty is different.

Traditionally unbeautiful things can evoke feelings of delight. For instance, I grew up near Coney Island, an amusement park in the southern-most tip of Brooklyn, New York. Even though most of it is tacky and dangerous, I continue to be attracted to the beauty of twinkling lights, and although it's not healthy food, I think it's magical to see sugar turn into candy floss! No surprise then that I loved putting broken mirror among the Italian silver tessera in my A train project, making that dismal place sparkle – and, at least for me, beautiful! It seems to me that we're not living in a very beautiful, ethical or delightful time. It is not that I want to give design a trivial role, but perhaps there simply could be more delight and playfulness – there is too much hubris and potential for damage in being inspiring. I do see people having a hunger for respite from the grind of the everyday, and the egregious behaviour in the world at large.

Ali Rashidi **graduated from California College of Arts and Crafts, USA and was designer and art director at University of California Publications before establishing his own design office. He moved to Iran in 1990 and co-founded Daarvag International, a communications company handling design and advertising projects for local and international clients including Unicef, the British Council and Unilever. A board member of the Iranian Graphic Designers Society, Rashidi is also international editor of** Neshan**, the first Iranian graphic design magazine.**
[Iranian, born 1953]

According to the Oxford English Dictionary**, 'good' means 'of high quality or acceptable standard'. To evaluate graphic design by these yardsticks is problematic; a universal definition does not exist, different cultures have varying and localised understandings of such terminology. If we consider works of graphic design to consist of two components – idea and execution – and if we agree that the essential part of any work is the idea or concept that engendered it, then it would be impossible to make an appraisal of the ideas that go into creating a graphic design piece based on universally agreed definitions. Each community has its own set of quality standards, informed by cultural and social values. To insist on a single set of standards is neither fair nor possible, and closes the door to the beauty of cultural and social diversity. We must acknowledge that credible appraisals are only possible if they are informed by the social and cultural values of the society in which the designer lives. Otherwise, the appraisal is a formalistic phenomenon, concerned only with the execution – as is the case in many international graphic design competitions.**

Poster
2001
A poster for the first Iranian graphic design group show. Rashidi is concerned with nurturing and promoting the emerging graphic design scene in Iran and developing its professional profile at home and abroad.

Luba Lukova graduated from the Academy of Fine Arts in Sofia before leaving Bulgaria in 1991 to live and work in New York. Her graphic art explores humanity's elemental themes and has appeared in publications including the New York Times and Time magazine. She received the Grand Prix Savignac for the World's Most Memorable Poster and the ICOGRADA Excellence Award. Lukova's work is widely exhibited, including solo exhibitions at UNESCO Paris. [American, born 1960]

I've always thought that other people, not me, should say whether I am good at what I do. Very often we designers think that the general public does not fully appreciate our profession. This is probably true, but the blame is with design itself – not with ordinary people who don't care about cool layouts, trendy typefaces, or superficial provocativeness. What people need from art and design are pieces that stir the emotions and haunt you, and make you think. This has never been easy to do. But work like this triggers a transformation of the audience's opinion of graphic design. People who have never cared about design will begin to notice it and need it. They may even steal the posters from the theatre lobby or tattoo a poster image on their skin. When something like this happens with my images, I take it as a sign that I might have done something good. Our audience wants to be moved and uplifted. This is what good design should do.

**Eco Crime
1997**
This award-winning poster is part of the Crime Series that Lukova designed for American magazine Nozone. Articulating the interdependence between humanity and nature, it memorably illustrates how in destroying nature we destroy ourselves.

Susanne Dechant trained at Grafische Lehr- und Versuchsanstalt, Vienna before founding her studio, Dechant Grafische Arbeiten, specialising in typography for book and editorial design. She is author of the digital typography guidebook Kursbuch Xpress and her projects include a recent campaign to promote car-sharing in Vienna for Verkehrsverbund Ost-Region, one of Austria's biggest public transport systems. Dechant is head of graphic design at Werbe Akademie, Vienna, and an academic consultant on feminist education and politics. She is Austrian delegate for the Association Typographique Internationale. [Austrian, born 1962]

'No', says my official voice. 'Yes', answers my inner, private voice. I guess not being a good designer does not imply being a bad one, and surely not an evil one! Good designers should use the powerful instrument of visual communication for the right things; isn't that the overall accepted definition? My first reaction is that I am not engaged enough to say I achieve this. But then I wonder do I want to be this kind of good designer? I am no missionary. Do I have to be a good designer? Isn't it enough not to design for radical parties, for senseless advertisements, for self-destructive sexist jokes? Good is perhaps something we should be, not something we must be. My ideals are far from reality. They revolve around ideas of political correctness and equality between genders, so maybe my aims are different to the general aims of good design. Perhaps I take the lesser evil by refraining from designing for advertising industries or marketing machines that conflict with my idea of the proper use of communication design. I try to live on okay jobs, doing okay design. I cannot do bad design for good ideas and I refrain from doing good design for silly ideas.

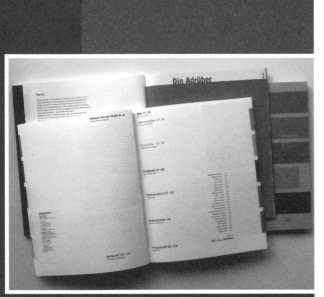

Catalogues
2000–04
Dechant has designed a series of catalogues showcasing student work for Werbe Akademie in Vienna, where she is head of graphic design. Each publication uses a range of print and production techniques to engage the reader and encourage interaction.

Section 2 concluded with a set of possible ethical principles. In Section 3 we explored how these might be applied in the practice of graphic design. In Section 4, 15 designers have considered what it means to be 'good'. Inevitably their answers were sometimes conflicting, but nevertheless there were also recurring themes. Here are some of them:

Qualitative language

Despite agreement that 'good' when applied to design is impossible to define easily, the understanding is that the term applies to both content and form. However, when evaluating design we generally focus on outcome, rather than the message or the client or designer intention. Michael Marriott called for extending our design vocabulary so that ethical issues can be explored more meaningfully.

Responsibility

Questioning the areas for which designers are truly responsible was a recurring theme. Contributors spoke about the simultaneous rewards and penalties of operating in our present economic system – recycling, waste and unnecessary mass production were identified as pressing ethical dilemmas. thomas.matthews argued that designers must be prepared to challenge client needs and expectations, while architect Billie Tsien focused on leaving a lasting and positive mark. Although most graphic design is ephemeral, each piece conveys a message and with this comes a responsibility. Simon Esterson suggested that categorising clients as 'clean' or not is simplistic – designers have to be inquisitive and honest with themselves about the important issues. Of all the contributors, photojournalist Chris de Bode confronts notions of truth most obviously in his work. He considered being true to the subjects of his pictures as his greatest responsibility.

Inclusion

Making design work that is accessible is an obvious area of social responsibility, but Sheila Levrant de Bretteville explored the notion of inclusion more broadly. She wants her work to give voice to those who are not represented, often working with small local communities as a result. Being ethical requires designers to be aware of collective and social responsibilities that are as much focused on helping or delighting the few as the many. De Bretteville is wary of the exclusivity of taking the moral high-ground and is keen to expose the ambiguities within ethics.

Humility

Oded Ezer described graphic design as occupying a space between need and fantasy – it certainly takes a humble but confident designer to be truly ethical. It requires us to recognise that on the whole, graphic design contributions are small – but not invaluable. It may also mean taking a stand against prevailing fashions, which is hard to do. As Simon Esterson said, you have to be a very good designer to be free of the designer ego.

Happiness

Crucial to ethics is the idea of engendering happiness in others. As Luba Lukova said, audiences want to be moved and uplifted – a valuable design outcome. Although implicit in many responses, some contributors were wary of the notion that their own happiness was valuable too. Acquisitiveness is often the root of unhappiness – Michael Marriott said he is lucky because little things make him happy. Billie Tsien commented that being ethical isn't meant to be easy and that struggle in itself is a good thing. Will Holder meanwhile described design as akin to a friend – someone who helps determine your ethos in life.

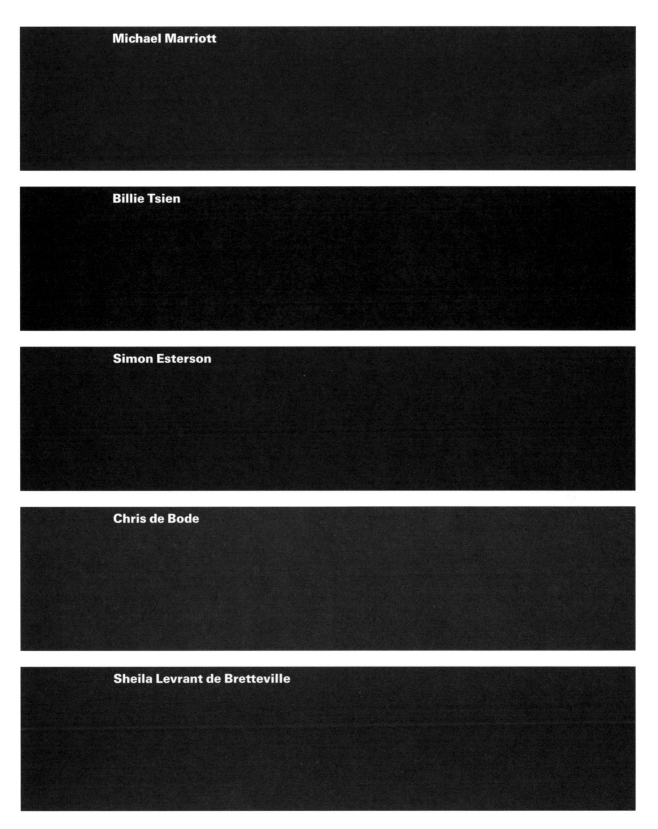

Michael Marriott

Billie Tsien

Simon Esterson

Chris de Bode

Sheila Levrant de Bretteville

Michael Marriott is interested by the essential nature of things. 'I still pull things out of skips or off the street because I'm interested in the form or how it's made.' Marriott is pragmatic, acknowledging that capitalism is 'a bit berserk now', but believing he is best employed making a difference from within.

1
Doubt Delight and Change/ Cedric Price
Design Museum, London
2005
A retrospective exhibition of the work of architect Cedric Price, designed in collaboration with graphic designer, Jon Hares. A shallow, wall-mounted, magnetic hanging system was used in conjunction with a low-budget, easy-to-assemble display.

2
Isambard Kingdom Brunel room for British Council
2003
Marriott used a standard industrial racking system as the architecture for this two storey, shed-like environment and furnished it with a diverse collection of British designed products.

3
Table Bench, prototype
2002
A dual height side table/bench, in homage to three existing small pieces of furniture designed by Max Bill, Achille Castiglioni and Le Corbusier.

4
Economy of Means
Camden Arts Centre, London
2004
An installation of 20 white tables, celebrating the simplicity and wonder of the trestle and similar ad-hoc support structures, inspired by a Robert Doisneau photograph of French pigeon fanciers.

5
Missed Day Bed, SCP
1998
A day bed sharing the same general form and dimensions of a standard single divan bed, but made from utilitarian yet luxurious materials; stainless steel legs and untreated natural leather upholstery, resulting in a subtle patina over time.

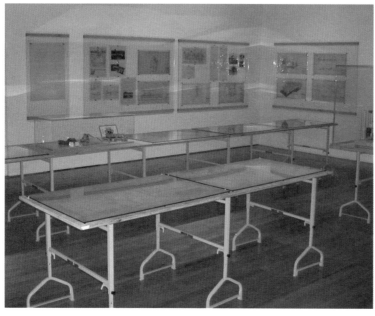

1
2 3

→ 114
Michael Marriott/ interview

4
5

8, 9, 10
**American Folk Art Museum
New York, USA**
completed 2001
The museum's façade is
sculptural in form and clad in
white bronze panels that catch
the sun along 53rd Street as it
rises and sets. Inside, a skylight
allows natural light to filter into
the galleries and lower levels
through openings at each floor.
A series of niches are built into
the structure so that visitors
encounter art in unexpected
and informal settings – making
each visit a personal journey.

Billie Tsien's approach to
architecture is characterised by her belief
that 'it is possible to make places on the earth
that can give a sense of grace to life'. She
and partner Tod Williams focus on what
they, as transient beings, can meaningfully
leave behind.

6, 7
**Neurosciences Research
Institute, California, USA**
completed 1995
The NSRI is a theoretical
and clinical research campus
for the study of the brain.
Tsien and her partner Williams
were keen to preserve the views
of the Santa Rosa Mountains
to the east, so the sloping site
was developed to keep
the buildings low and firmly
engaged with the land. Every
part of the Institute – from
the buildings and the landscape
to the furniture and the
tapestry – has been designed
to form a coherent and serene
environment, a monastery
for science.

6 7

→ 122
**Billie Tsien/
interview**

8 9 10

Simon Esterson specialises
in editorial design – 'a little separate world
outside the mainstream of graphic design'.
Magazines and newspapers are funded
through advertising, so despite the serious
nature of the material he designs, Esterson
discusses it as a commercial enterprise
that necessitates some ethical compromise.

11–15
**Front and back cover,
spreads and section opener
of Eye magazine**
issue 60, summer 2006
Eye is a quarterly magazine
about graphic design. The
design needs to present a
variety of different visual
material clearly to an image-
conscious audience. Esterson
as art director and designers
Jay Prynne and Kucha Swara
consider it vital to work closely
with the authors and editor
John L Walters.

16
**Front page of
NZZ am Sonntag**
2004
One of Europe's oldest daily
papers, the Swiss-based
Neue Zurcher Zeitung wanted
to launch a Sunday newspaper
in the Berliner format. Simon
Esterson and Mark Porter were
appointed as art directors and
responded positively to the
brief to design a paper that
was modern, but authoritative.

11

→ 126
**Simon Esterson/
interview**

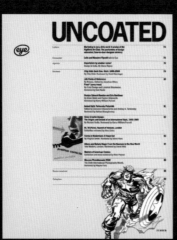

16

12–15

Simon Esterson argues that it is simplistic to assume all corporate clients are 'bad'. Organisations that rely on public revenue are largely funded via taxes on business and even individual charity donations may not be 'clean'. A prerequisite to ethical awareness is an acknowledgement of the complexity of the issues involved.

17–19
Cover and spreads,
New Statesman
redesigned June 2006
Stephen Coates and Simon Esterson worked as consultants with Art Director David Gibbons and proposed a cover system that breaks away from the bleed image with the type overprinting format that most magazines use. Appealing to an audience of writers, inside spreads use a few large pictures and well-presented text.

20
Le Temps
redesigned June 2005
Esterson worked as Art Director with Jon Hill on this typographic overhaul of the Geneva-based Swiss daily paper. They applied rigorous thinking and chose a slightly condensed face, Unger's Coranto, to accommodate its long headlines.

17–19

→ 126
**Simon Esterson/
interview**

J.A. 1211 Genève 2 | www.letemps.ch

LE TEMPS

Cinéma
«Locataires», chef-d'œuvre coréen qui a fait pleurer Venise *Page 40*

Portrait
Mark Malloch Brown, le très influent chef de cabinet de Kofi Annan *Page 17*

Robe de mariée
Que choisir pour son deuxième mariage? Tendances et retour sur Camilla *Page 44*

ÉCONOMIE & FINANCE

Presse La croissance d'Edipresse et de Ringier passe par l'étranger: 23, 24

Enquête L'ONU a de sérieux doutes sur la gestion de l'OMPI à Genève: 23

Etats-Unis Le déficit attendu: 33

Mercredi 13 avril 2005 | N° 2156 — QUOTIDIEN SUISSE ÉDITÉ À GENÈVE — CHF 2.50, France € 2.20

L'essentiel

International

La campagne électorale choc des Tories
En Grande-Bretagne, les conservateurs font de l'immigration le thème central de leur campagne et espèrent ainsi déstabiliser les travaillistes de Tony Blair *Page 4*

Reportage dans les montagnes d'Aceh
Alors que les pourparlers ont repris hier en Finlande, notre envoyé spécial raconte comment les rebelles vivent la fragile trêve humanitaire *Page 6*

Suisse

Les finances des CFF plombées par les retraites
Malgré une progression du trafic voyageurs et marchandises, l'ancienne régie est confrontée aux difficultés de sa caisse de retraite *Page 7*

Régions

La gauche veut réinstaurer le consensus à Neuchâtel
Sous la houlette de Jean Studer, socialistes et Verts sacrifient Didier Berberat pour rétablir un équilibre politique *Page 10*

Sports

Nouvelle inculpation contre Marc Roger
Déjà prévenu de gestion déloyale, abus de confiance et de banqueroute frauduleuse, l'ex-président du Servette FC a été inculpé hier de faux dans les titres dans le cadre de la faillite du club. *Page 15*

Culture

Le programme complet du Montreux Jazz Festival
De Crosby, Stills & Nash à Juliette Gréco en passant par la reine du hip-hop Lauryn Hill, le poète Elvis Costello et l'excentrique Alice Cooper, gros plan sur la 39e édition qui se déroulera du 1er au 16 juillet. *Page 41*

L'anglais devient la langue de dialogue entre les Suisses

Langues Les régions sont de plus en plus centrées sur leur langue. Et l'anglais s'impose

La germanisation de la Suisse latine n'aura pas lieu: le français et l'italien se portent à merveille sur leur territoire. L'envahissement linguistique étranger non plus: contrairement à tous les pronostics, la part des allophones sur notre territoire n'a pas varié depuis dix ans. Présentée hier à Ber

ne, l'analyse du dernier recensement fédéral laisse apparaître un futur paysage linguistique helvétique menacé par un autre danger: on y voit des régions linguistiquement fortes, toujours plus homogènes et imperméables au quadrilinguisme national. Tellement homogènes et imper

méables qu'elles tendent à communiquer entre elles en anglais.

L'utilisation de l'anglais dans la vie active est en effet en augmentation, tandis que stagnent ou régressent les langues nationales hors de leur territoire. Elles sont pourtant utiles au travail, notamment dans les emplois moins qua

lifiés, note Georges Lüdi, professeur de linguistique française à l'université de Bâle et coauteur de l'analyse des données du recensement: ainsi, si l'école mise sur l'anglais, les jeunes défavorisés le seront encore plus.

Parmi les langues nationales, l'allemand et le français se por

tent bien. En revanche, l'italien est en recul et le romanche agonise. Par ailleurs, en raison des origines des nouvelles populations immigrées, les langues étrangères parlées en Suisse sont en nette progression, en particulier le serbo-croate.

▶ *Page 3*

Alinghi dévoile ses quartiers généraux à Valence

Ernesto Bertarelli a dévoilé hier à Valence la base nautique du Team Alinghi, qui défendra son titre de détenteur de la Coupe de l'America. Les moyens investis sont considérables et à la hauteur d'une compétition qui draine les plus grandes fortunes du monde. ▶ *Page 15*

Hans Küng dénonce l'inquisition

Cette semaine est cruciale pour l'élection du futur pape. Les cardinaux, qui ont pratiquement tous été élus par Jean Paul II, doivent définir le profil du prochain souverain pontife. Dans cette configuration, des réformes sont-elles possibles?

Le théologien Hans Küng se montre très critique à l'égard de la curie. Dans une interview accordée au *Temps*, il estime que l'administration du Vatican tente d'empêcher le futur pape de s'écarter de la ligne de Jean Paul II.

Par le passé, ce théologien lucernois s'est attiré les foudres de la hiérarchie catholique pour ses prises de position virulentes contre le pontificat du pape défunt. Il affirme aujourd'hui que l'Eglise doit «abolir l'inquisition représentée par le cardinal Joseph Ratzinger» et estime qu'en faisant campagne pour la canonisation de Jean Paul II, la curie cherche à empêcher toute remise en question de son pontificat.

▶ *Page 43*

A nos lecteurs, par Stéphane Garelli*

Le journal dont la Suisse romande a besoin

Le 21 août 1849, Victor Hugo fait le discours d'ouverture du premier Congrès de la Paix à Paris; il fera aussi celui du deuxième, 20 ans plus tard à... Lausanne. «Un jour viendra où il n'y aura plus d'autres champs de bataille que les marchés s'ouvrant au commerce et les esprits s'ouvrant aux idées.» Nous n'y sommes pas encore. Pourtant les débats d'idées et l'économie ponctuent notre société moderne. *Le Temps* veut en être le témoin.

Votre journal prend son second souffle. Le premier, qui a vu sa création, était celui de la créativité et des incertitudes. Les actionnaires et les collaborateurs du journal ont fait le pari qu'il y

avait dans notre petit bout de pays une place pour ce que les Anglo-Saxons appellent un «quality papers». Dans une société parfois plus préoccupée par le pain et les jeux et où le réflexe remplace souvent la réflexion, c'était pourtant risqué. Ce pari a pourtant réussi. *Le Temps* est devenu en quelques années le journal suisse de référence de langue française, un des rares connus à l'étranger. L'année dernière, ses comptes furent équilibrés.

Mais cela ne suffit pas. Informer professionnellement, s'adresser à l'intelligence ou à l'esprit critique des lecteurs ne font pas d'un journal une institution. Dans une démocratie, un journal comme

Le Temps doit être le moyen privilégié pour qu'une société se parle à elle-même. Le second souffle du *Temps* se caractérise par une plus grande ouverture aux idées, aux débats, aux grandes décisions, à tout ce qui vous permet d'être mieux informés, de mieux réfléchir, de mieux prendre position.

Avoir des ambitions implique aussi des responsabilités: la rigueur des analyses, la séparation entre les faits et les opinions. Mais *Le Temps*, c'est aussi un état d'esprit que nous voulons maintenir et développer. L'information et le débat d'idées doivent être vifs, incisifs, précis, mais le respect des personnes, acteurs ou lecteurs,

doit être absolu. Ce sera notre seul parti pris.

Vous nous consacrez, en moyenne, 30 minutes par jour, 30 minutes où l'important doit prendre le pas sur l'urgent. Durant cet espace de temps, ce journal a l'ambition d'être votre fenêtre sur le monde des événements, des personnes et des idées. Ces idées qui nous font avancer. Car il y a une chose plus forte que toutes les armées du monde, c'est une idée dont le temps est venu. Cela aurait pu être la devise du *Temps*. C'est aussi du Victor Hugo...

▶ *Pages 20 et 21*

*Président du conseil d'administration du «Temps»

Météo du jour

Matinée 5° — Après-midi 15°

www.letemps.ch/forum
Donnez votre avis à propos de notre nouvelle formule

9 771423 396001

Chris de Bode finds working as a photojournalist can be distressing and lonely, but his belief in the power of striking and beautiful images as a means of telling the truth remains paramount. 'People are struck by the directness of my way of communicating, so in some sense I succeed in transmitting the message.'

21
Three Gorges Dam, China
2001
This will be the biggest hydroelectric dam in the world, supplying 11 per cent of China's energy. Up to 1.3 million residents will be relocated to make way for the new lake.

22
Tour de Qatar
2001
Qatari women watch cyclists in the first Tour de Qatar. There were bemused glances from locals as bicycles are a rare sight in the desert.

23
Cali, Colombia
2003
Competitors in the 53rd Vuelta a Colombia flash past spectators. The race took place amid civil war and violence – the entire route was guarded by armed Colombian soldiers.

24
Lira, Uganda
2004
Sandra Abeja is a malnourished orphan brought to MSF's therapeutic feeding centre by her grandfather after her parents were killed by the Lord's Resistance Army. Northern Uganda has been described as the 'largest neglected humanitarian emergency in the world'.

25
Chimbiri, Ethiopia
2005
A classroom in Chimbiri school, one of the best in the region, has one desk for every four students. Schools do not exist in many rural areas, even though education is compulsory in Ethiopia.

21
22 23

→ 132
Chris de Bode/ interview

Sheila Levrant de Bretteville's work as a graphic designer, educator and public artist stimulates awareness of the people, subjects and voices dominant culture often fails to accommodate. 'My thoughts move toward ways of making that provide models for inclusion… how I can bring those at the periphery into public view.'

26–29
**Remembering old Little Tokyo
Los Angeles, USA**
1995
De Bretteville used quotes from three generations of inhabitants in the new pavement on the oldest commercial street in LA. Alternating coloured strips define the narrow building lots, amid images of trunks brought here by the first generation of immigrants and used again when they were forced to leave the neighbourhood. Along the doorways, a timeline delivers the hidden history of Japanese and African Americans. Use of the buildings is shown in brass lettering – which will remain bright only if in constant use – the details of the removal of people of Japanese descent in the 1940s are in stainless steel.

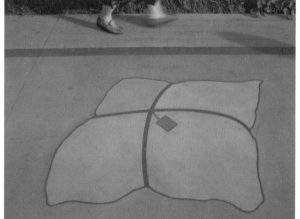

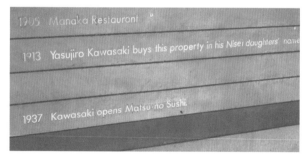

1905 Manaka Restaurant

1913 Yasujiro Kawasaki buys this property in his Nisei daughters' name

1937 Kawasaki opens Matsu-no Sushi.

26–28

→ 136
**Sheila Levrant de Bretteville/
interview**

1941 · FBI raids Issei associations for evidence of disloyalty.

Sheila Levrant de Bretteville
leaves space in her work to reflect the
ambiguity of life. 'It is important to remember
that ethical considerations aren't clear-cut
and are often contingent inventions! I use
question marks or ellipses in my work to imply
this lack, that everything is not resolved…'

30–32
**Out to lunch… Back to work…
Rhode Island, USA
2000**
The Rhode Island Department
of Labor and Training wanted to
develop a courtyard for their
workers and local residents
within newly renovated workhouse buildings. De Bretteville
and colleague Henk vanAssen
placed chairs and tables within
a newly planted crab apple
orchard, reminiscent of the trees
on site when the buildings
were first put up by workhouse
inmates. The granite seats carry
messages, cushions are available
from the cafeteria on cold days,
and 10,000 different combinations
of sentences about work
and working are etched into
the 'lazy Susan' table.

33, 34
**At the start… At long last…
New York, USA
1999**
At the tip of Manhattan
is the 207th street terminus
of the A train, New York's
longest subway line.
Throughout the station are
pieces of de Bretteville's
work, each designed to enrich
and sparkle as they tell the
varied history of music,
immigration, ethnicity,
economic survival and risk
at this site. The ellipsis is used
to emphasise the open-ended
nature of travel, and indeed
life. Etched into the new
stainless steel handrail is
Billy Strayhorn's jazz classic
Take the A Train.

30
31 32

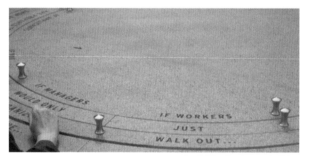

→ 136
**Sheila Levrant de Bretteville/
interview**

Good:
An introduction to ethics in graphic design
Section 5: Doing good/practical considerations
Rupert Bassett/Lynne Elvins +
**Ken Garland/Violetta Boxill/Pat Kahn/
Dan Eatock/**Dave Shaw photography

LE

We have both worked for a consultancy that advises large businesses about sustainability. We have design backgrounds and it was clear to us that designers weren't being included enough in the debate, so we set up our own consultancy – A420 – and developed Sustainability Issue Mapping to do just that. Sustainable design can contribute to a more sustainable world – one that will not only last, but brings benefits to society at large. The problem is that sustainability is quite complicated. It's not just some niche subject about recycling. Our maps are an introduction to it.

RB

We wanted to show that every designer has the potential to produce more sustainable design with every project they tackle. But to engage designers it was essential that we explained it in a systematic and visually dynamic way.

LE

Basically, we didn't want to write another 50-page report that no one would read.

RB

So, we developed the methodology and then designed and printed our guide to sustainable design. It's a big fold-out format showing a series of maps. Each map is made up of coloured squares with issues on them. The set of issues is not definitive, but the idea is that the squares nearer the middle of a map are the most important.

LE

In order to make sustainability simpler to understand, we broke it down into three parts: <u>contexts</u>, <u>agendas</u> and <u>issues</u>.

RB

Understanding the overall context in which design operates is vital because design does not exist in isolation. So, the context maps demonstrate how design is a small part of business and that business is a part of the world. All three are linked. For designers to understand their role, it's important that they make a connection between creating design work and creating more sustainable businesses, which in turn create a more sustainable world.

LE

Within the contexts are four agendas: <u>financial</u>, <u>social</u>, <u>environmental</u> and <u>personal</u>. Sustainable design is about balancing these agendas.

RB

This isn't easy because they are in constant conflict with each other and are being driven by many different issues, from 'reducing pollution' to 'making profit'. By mapping the issues against the four agenda axes, we can show which are most important to each project and which ones might be missing.

LE

Being more sustainable is about aiming for balance across the four agendas. The overall function of Sustainability Issue Mapping is that it reveals imbalances. Our printed version of the design issues map isn't definitive. When we use it with designers we supply them with blank squares, as well as a set with preprinted words. They often come up with new issues and reorder them too.

RB

But the result is that designers can clearly see what issues they need to focus on, in order to make their design work more sustainable.

LE

When we discuss our work on sustainable design we are often asked, 'Could you call this ethical design?'. Our answer is, of course, yes, and that we could also frame the subject as 'moral', 'responsible' or even 'good' design. Sustainable design is often thought to be only about the environment, but it is much wider than that. It's about balancing environmental and social responsibilities against financial pressures and personal desires – balancing everything in a more informed and responsible way for a better quality of life.

RB

Ultimately these issues shouldn't require any separate labelling. Instead, they should be a generally accepted part of 'normal design'. But, for a number of reasons, we are a long way from that.

LE

So when we were asked to analyse the work of graphic designers for this book, we were confident that our Sustainability Issue Mapping would do the job because 'sustainable design' is so closely related to the subject of 'ethical design'.

RB

We usually apply our thinking to individual design projects rather than people, but felt that we should also be able to assess what general considerations designers were making by asking them about the financial, social, environmental and personal issues that they are confronted with when working.

LE

We did not need to know if they recycled their bottles at home or if they regularly bought the **Big Issue**. What we wanted to get to was a practical sense of which issues were coming into play in their working lives as designers.

RB

Armed with blank Sustainability Issue Maps and lists of issues, we put ourselves in the hands of four very different designers. The results were fascinating and far more complex than we were initially prepared for. Naïvely perhaps, we underestimated just how unique and subjective the responses would be when the spotlight is put on to a person rather than a project.

LE

At times, we concluded that it may be impossible to compare people objectively when the factors involved are so complex. But in the end the results gave us a much clearer idea of how different designers have to deal with 'ethics'. Not just in relation to their own feelings on the subject, but in terms of the reality of their influence as a designer, their client expectations and their place in the world.

RB

What follows are the results of those four discussions, our reactions to them and the resulting issue maps.

Using the large fold-out map for reference, Lynne Elvins assembles a new map. When Bassett and Elvins work with designers they supply blank squares, as well as a set with preprinted words, so that new issues can be added and existing issues can be reordered.

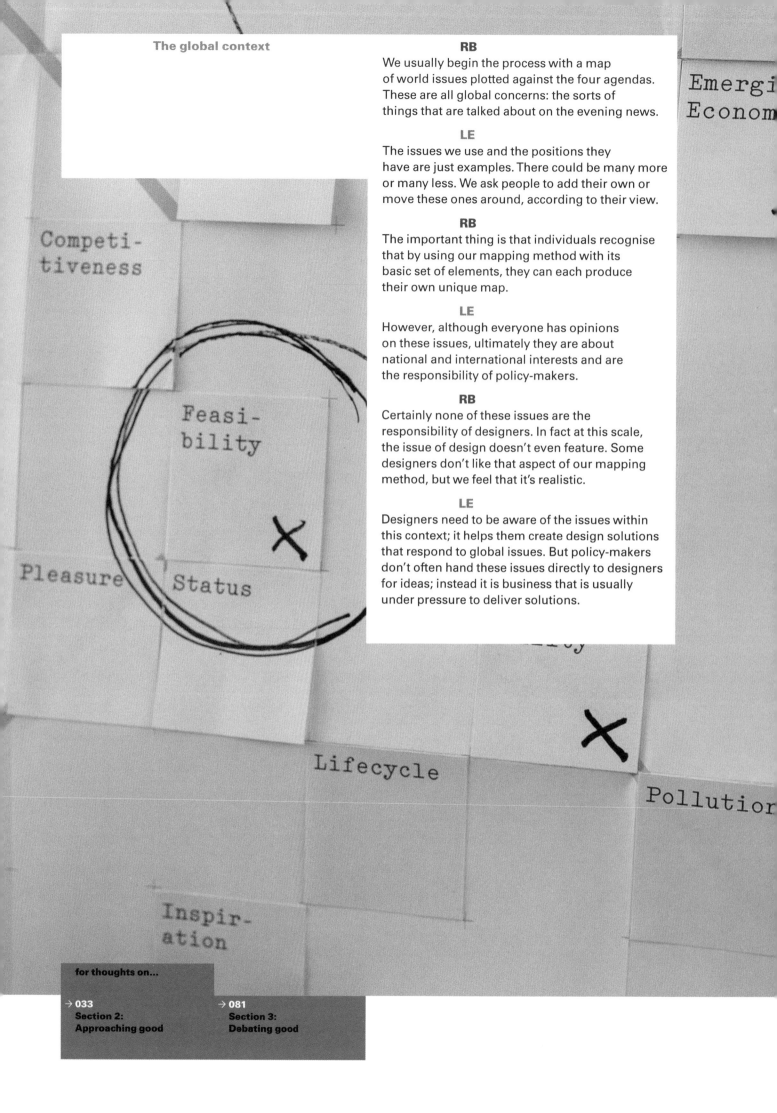

RB
We usually begin the process with a map of world issues plotted against the four agendas. These are all global concerns: the sorts of things that are talked about on the evening news.

LE
The issues we use and the positions they have are just examples. There could be many more or many less. We ask people to add their own or move these ones around, according to their view.

RB
The important thing is that individuals recognise that by using our mapping method with its basic set of elements, they can each produce their own unique map.

LE
However, although everyone has opinions on these issues, ultimately they are about national and international interests and are the responsibility of policy-makers.

RB
Certainly none of these issues are the responsibility of designers. In fact at this scale, the issue of design doesn't even feature. Some designers don't like that aspect of our mapping method, but we feel that it's realistic.

LE
Designers need to be aware of the issues within this context; it helps them create design solutions that respond to global issues. But policy-makers don't often hand these issues directly to designers for ideas; instead it is business that is usually under pressure to deliver solutions.

Competi-
tiveness

Feasi-
bility

Pleasure   Status

Lifecycle

Pollutior

Emergi
Econom

Inspir-
ation

for thoughts on...

→ 033
Section 2:
Approaching good

→ 081
Section 3:
Debating good

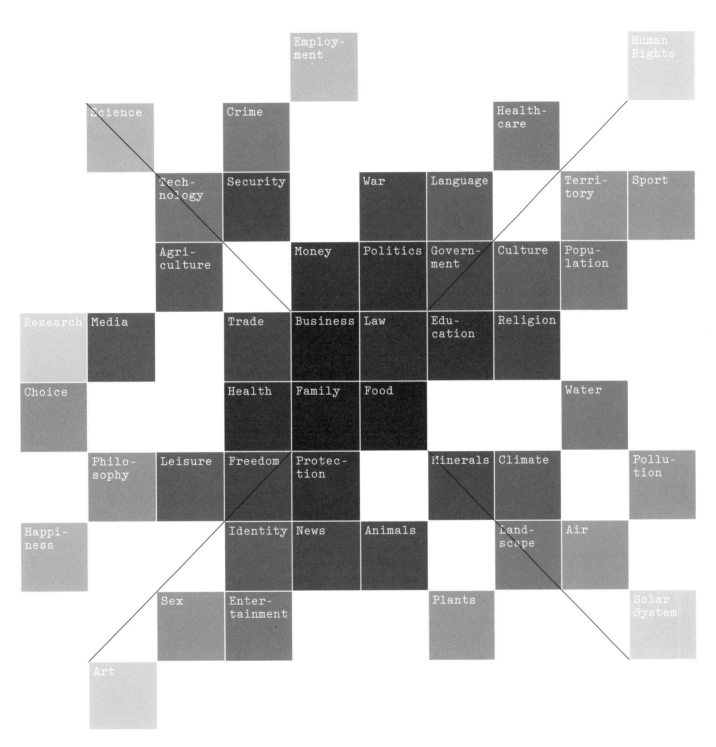

An example of how a global context map might look. Issues are grouped according to the four agendas – financial, social, personal and environmental – with darker squares indicating the issues felt to be the most important to the map maker.

RB

When we 'zoom in' on the issue of business, it becomes an entire context in its own right. The map shown is again only an example of how business issues might be arranged.

LE

In this context, issues relate to the management of organisations and are the responsibility of business managers.

RB

At this scale, design becomes visible, but it is just one of many other issues. However, it does have the potential to occupy an important central position.

LE

Again, some designers have a real problem with this. Seeing their whole world as a small part of a bigger business is difficult to deal with.

RB

An important feature of the example is that it shows an imbalance weighted, not surprisingly, towards the financial agenda.

LE

The more designers understand business issues, the better they can respond to the increasing demands of new business strategies.

for thoughts on...

→ **081**
Section 3:
Debating good

→ **113**
Section 4:
Being good

An example of how a business context map might look. Issues are grouped according to the four agendas – financial, social, personal and environmental – with darker squares indicating the issues felt to be the most important to the map maker.

Financial   Social

Personal   Environmental

Governance							Dis-closure
Risk	Effi-ciency				Account-ability		
R&D	Tech-nology		Invest-ment		Pensions	Trade Unions	Social Respons-ibility
Distri-bution	Dead-lines	Strategy	Compet-ition		Stan-dards	Health & Safety	
Know-ledge	Sales	Share-holders	Manage-ment	Legis-lation			
Brand Value	Market-ing	PR	Pro-duction		Supply Chains		
Graphic Design	Customer		Facil-ities		Location		
Employ-ees		Raw Material					
Human Resource							
Training							

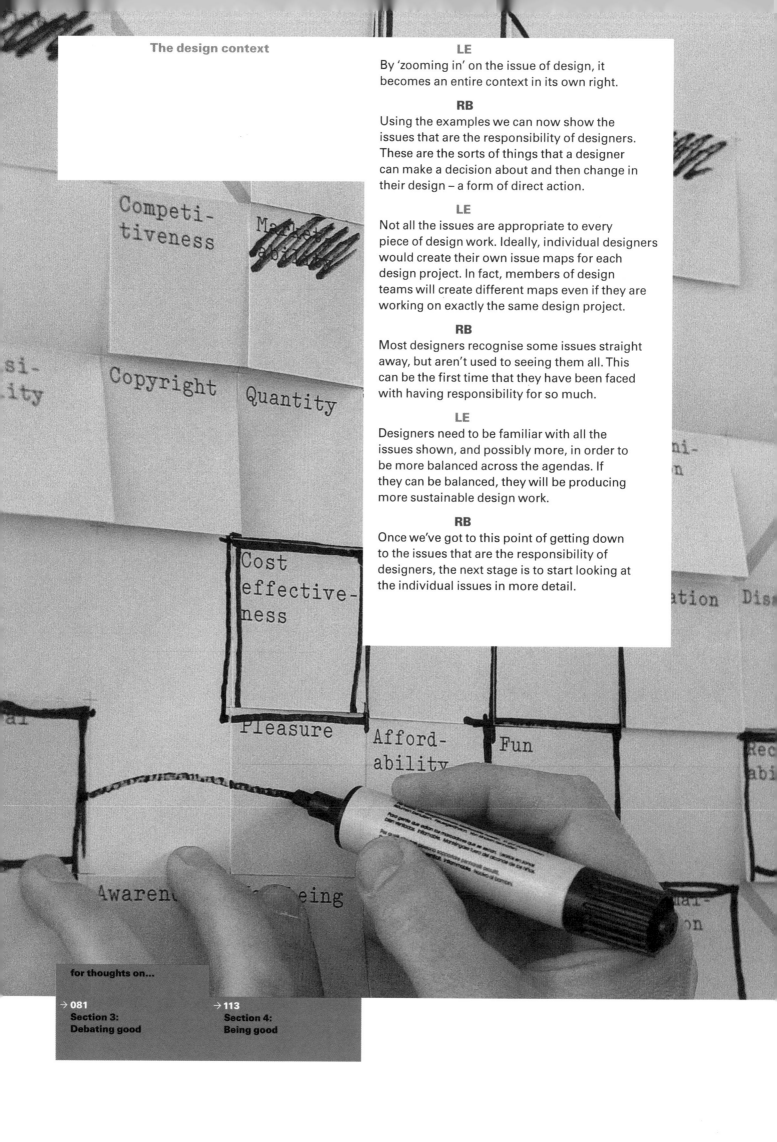

LE

By 'zooming in' on the issue of design, it becomes an entire context in its own right.

RB

Using the examples we can now show the issues that are the responsibility of designers. These are the sorts of things that a designer can make a decision about and then change in their design – a form of direct action.

LE

Not all the issues are appropriate to every piece of design work. Ideally, individual designers would create their own issue maps for each design project. In fact, members of design teams will create different maps even if they are working on exactly the same design project.

RB

Most designers recognise some issues straight away, but aren't used to seeing them all. This can be the first time that they have been faced with having responsibility for so much.

LE

Designers need to be familiar with all the issues shown, and possibly more, in order to be more balanced across the agendas. If they can be balanced, they will be producing more sustainable design work.

RB

Once we've got to this point of getting down to the issues that are the responsibility of designers, the next stage is to start looking at the individual issues in more detail.

for thoughts on...

→ **081**
Section 3:
Debating good

→ **113**
Section 4:
Being good

Financial   Social
Personal   Environmental

An example of how a design context map might look. Issues are grouped according to the four agendas – financial, social, personal and environmental – with darker squares indicating the issues felt to be the most important to the map maker.

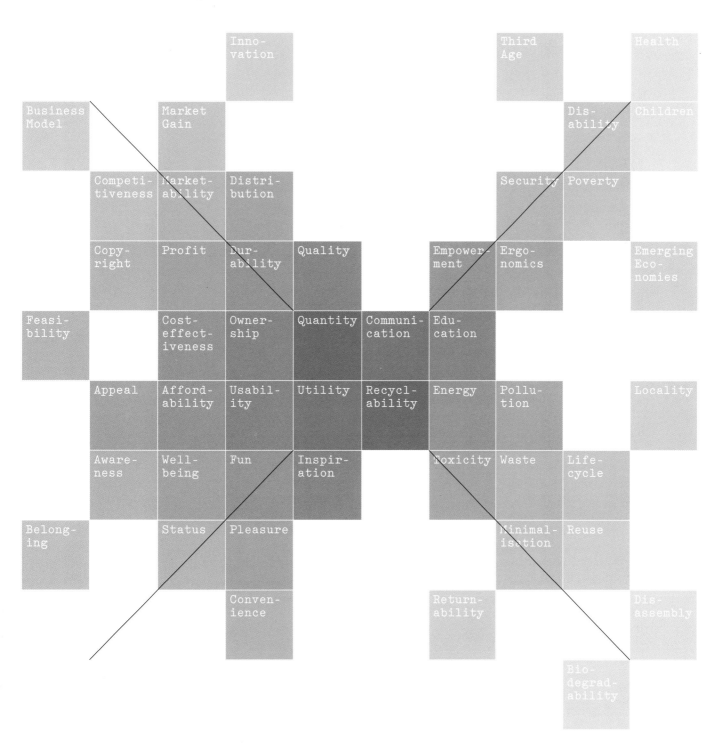

Creating financially viable
work focuses on the design
issues that affect the costs
of distribution and production.
The parameters are most
likely to be set by clients,
but designers may be able
to suggest alternative
approaches if they are aware
of the client's aims, have
a good relationship with the
client and are involved in
the briefing process early
enough. Ultimately, this
agenda is driven by an
increasingly competitive
market. But, if designers focus
too much on cost-cutting
or profit-making, the danger
is that the results will be
uninspiring and bland.

Innovation

Is your design
really something
new?

Feasibility

Is your design
realistic in
terms of
production?

Distribution

How will sizes
and weights of
the finished
piece of design
affect
distribution
costs?

Competitiveness

Will your design
surpass the
market leader
rather than
imitate it?

Marketability

Do you really
know your target
audience?

Copyright

Do you know that
you have not
copied or taken
unfair advantage
of other people's
ideas?

Profit

Do you know how
much money you
are aiming to
make for yourself
and your client?

Quality

Have you
clarified the
quality
expectations of
your client?

Appeal

Will your design
be wanted? Will
it be kept and
adored for years
to come?

Cost-
effectiveness

Have your design
specifications
been made to
maximise
the efficiency of
production?

Ownership

Do you know who
will own your
design? Have you
sought legal
advice and
secured a written
contract?

Quantity

Have you
understood the
creation process,
whether mass
produced or
individually
crafted?

for thoughts on...

→ 036
**Anthony Grayling
on the distorting nature
of money**

→ 056, 057
**Richard Holloway
on the free market**

→ 116–117
**Michael Marriott
on capitalism
and sustainability**

→ 137
**Sheila Levrant de Bretteville
on inclusion**

The social agenda
The overall question posed by this agenda is whether the finished design benefits society as a whole. Graphic designers don't usually dictate content, but they can decide whether they work for clients who are communicating something 'good' for society. Where should designers draw the line and why? These decisions are determined by the individual designer's sense of what is right or wrong. Given cultural and political differences arriving at a universally held consensus is practically impossible. For those who want it, work for good causes is there, but this often means working to tight budgets and within creatively restrictive briefs.

Security

Will the content help people stay safe?

Poverty

Does the content encourage unnecessary spending?

Children

Will your design encourage children to learn and develop positively?

Empowerment

Will the content help empower people?

Health

Will the content aid or encourage physical well-being?

Third Age

Have you chosen type sizes, colours or layouts that are legible to older people?

Education

Will the content educate in a positive way?

Communication

Will your design communicate something positive to its readers?

Disability

Have you chosen typefaces, sizes or colours that are legible to people with visual or other impairments?

Glossary of ethical thought

The personal agenda
Creating personally desirable
design work is about fulfilling
the dreams and desires
of the individual consumer.
Graphic designers are often
asked to address the latest
trends or use the latest
technology. Pressure comes
from end-users and their peers,
driven by ever-changing
fashions in consumer culture.
These issues are also dictated
by the form and function of the
design work – an instruction
manual for a mobile phone will
be different from its marketing
campaign or its onscreen
interface. But designers also
bring their own personal
preferences and often find it
hard to objectively design
for others.

Affordability

Will your design
be priced fairly
for what it is
and the job it
does?

Usability

Will your design
be legible to
read and simple
to understand?

Utility

Does your design
offer a useful
function? Is it
more than
something that
just looks good?

Awareness

Will your design
increase the
reader's
understanding
about something
they did not
know?

Fun

Will your design
make the end-user
laugh?

Convenience

Will your design
be easy to get
hold of for
everyone who
might need it?

Status

Will your design
be flaunted? Will
it be something
owned with pride?

Pleasure

Will your design
be sensuous to
touch and see?

Inspiration

Will your design
encourage end-
users to do or
think something
new?

for thoughts on...

→ **038–040**
Anthony Grayling
on happiness, beauty and
quality of life

→ **094–099**
Work and happiness

→ **185**
Pat Kahn
on being useful

Recyclability	**Energy**	**Pollution**		**Emerging Economies**

Recyclability

Can your design be recycled if it is laminated, coated or bound with non-recyclable materials?

Energy

How much energy will be used in the paper-making, printing and distribution of your design?

Pollution

How many harmful VOCs are connected to solvents in your inks?

Emerging Economies

Is your printer exploiting third world workers?

Toxicity

Is the chlorine used to whiten your paper linked with cancer causing dioxins?

Waste

How much water is used in your print process?

Minimalisation

Can you adjust the design so that the minimal amount of paper is used?

Biodegradability

How biodegradable are the papers or inks that you specify?

Returnability

Could your piece of graphic design be returned for recycling or reuse when it is finished with?

The environmental agenda
Environmentally responsible design is about considering the natural resources depleted in the production process. These issues are relatively new, but their acceptability is growing, driven by an increasing awareness of our impact on the planet. Designers are questioning the necessity of some of what they produce. In graphic design, there are concerns about printing processes, paper production and waste. By asking questions of stock suppliers and printers, designers can make a real difference – but the authority to specify paper or printers may not always lie with designers. However, clients are under increasing pressure to meet environmental standards so opportunities to discuss these issues are growing. It is no longer the case that awareness of environmental concerns need result in predictably eco-friendly solutions.

Glossary of ethical thought

→ 067
Aristotelianism

→ 073
Virtue ethics

Ken Garland trained at the Central School of Art and Crafts, London, UK and became art editor of Design magazine before starting his own studio, Ken Garland and Associates. Renowned for his fierce independence and inclusive view of the world, Garland is a designer, photographer and writer and his practice includes the design of educational games for Galt Toys, posters for the Campaign for Nuclear Disarmament and information graphics for the Ministry of Technology. He published the original First Things First manifesto in 1964 and was a co-signatory of the revised manifesto in 2000. Aesthetically broad and intellectually curious, his approach to work is defined by his aspiration to be faithful to its subject. [British, born 1929]

Violetta Boxill studied at Middlesex University and the Royal College of Art, London, UK. After graduating she co-founded Alexander Boxill Design, a small independent practice that she continues to run. Her eclectic work includes the design and art direction of icon magazine, of which she is currently Creative Director, the re-design of Design, the journal of the Design Council, and the identity for the Africa Remix exhibition at the Hayward Gallery, London. She has worked for many clients in the cultural sector including the London Design Festival, the Institute of Contemporary Arts and Wallpaper* magazine. In 2004 she was named Designer of The Year at the Independent Publishing Awards. [British, born 1970]

Pat Kahn began her working life in the USA as a calligrapher. On arrival in Britain she undertook postgraduate study with Nicolete Gray in the history of lettering at the Central School of Art and Design. After working in community printing and trade typesetting, she became – and remains – a London-based typographer and publication designer. Her clients are voluntary sector organisations and campaigning groups. Kahn enjoys the humdrum world of text typography and hates re-branding. She is a member of the Letter Exchange, a group of practitioners from across the lettering arts and writes web and arts reviews for Forum, the Letter Exchange magazine. Kahn also makes collages, reads voraciously and is currently writing a cookbook.

[Kahn declined to provide her year of birth and nationality, noting the current fashion for unwarranted data collection by governmental and commercial organisations and consequent creation of non-essential data pools.]

Dan Eatock is a graduate of Ravensbourne College of Design and Communication and the Royal College of Art, London, UK. He worked as an intern at the Walker Art Centre in Minneapolis, USA before establishing Foundation 33, a multi-disciplinary practice that later merged with creative agency boymeetsgirl. He recently formed Eatock Ltd, an independent art and design studio, where his entrepreneurial approach to authorship and his adherence to the integrity of ideas are applied to commercial design work and contemporary art projects. His varied portfolio includes the creation of the world's largest signed and numbered limited edition artwork and the ongoing design and development of the Big Brother identity for Channel 4. [British, born 1975]

**Drain grating in city centre
Belfast, Northern Ireland
1999**
On Friday 3 March 1978
Garland watched as a soldier
and female security guard
were shot by three gunmen
masquerading as Arabs
at a student rag day parade.
As they lay dying, their
blood trickled through this
grating to the city drains
below. Twenty-one years
later, Garland photographed
the same drain, this time
displaying the colourful
residue of celebration.

**Golf course sprinkler
Palm Springs, California,
USA
1998**
With an average annual rainfall
of five inches, and minimal
humidity, Palm Springs would
turn from green to brown
within 72 hours if these
sprinklers failed. But looking
at Garland's photograph we
can't help but question such
profligate water usage. The
numbers on the sprinkler head
refer to distances from players'
tees – more significant data to
the users of the course than
the rate of water consumption
and projected dates of
its inevitable exhaustion.

KG

One way I use to discuss ethics or sustainability is by using photographic metaphors. You can present a beautiful image to get people's attention. Some are easy to grasp and I get an 'oh yes' response. First the viewer sees a fun photograph and then they gradually get the wider picture and see what I'm on about, but relating it to their own design careers or study is a different matter. They may identify with the sprinkler design and sneer at the wasteful community of Palm Springs, California. That's okay, but what are you going to do about it as a designer, where do you go from there? What we are left with is saying to designers, 'What would you do as your tiny little contribution within all these problems?'. Unfortunately that doesn't make it easy for designers to feel powerful, and everyone has to feel empowered to make changes.

The reality for me is that my vote and my political actions are probably more valuable than anything I can do as a designer. I recall Buckminster Fuller once saying that if designers had control of world events instead of politicians they could solve world problems in a decade. This is ridiculous. If designers start tackling political situations they become politicians. You can't solve things by standing on the corner and shouting 'vote designers'.

But how do we embark on change when we don't seem to have convictions, either in our design attitudes, our political attitudes or our religious attitudes? It isn't possible. It's not about professional ethics, but personal morality, and that comes from our backgrounds and upbringing. All designers are quite likely to have some kind of moral position in relation to their work. Some of us have more of it and some have less. Young people are concerned and anxious about their future. It's all very well talking about ethics, sustainability or politics, but they've also got to face their future with hard-nosed employers or clients – and design is a buyer's market.

If there are people in business talking about sustainability, that's good, but do they really, really believe in this? Can they convince their shareholders? Business managers need quick return, and as for sustainability, excuse me, no thanks. I am a sceptic on these matters. What I am looking for is a change of heart. I don't trust the actions of people who are doing it because if they don't somebody is just going to jump down their neck. I do believe in controls, but if it doesn't involve a change of heart, we're not going to get a full-blooded response.

We have to take a pragmatic view. Start with the real world, not the ideal world, and we'll see how we can approach an ideal world from the real world. We mustn't give up. The temptation to slip into a cynical position on these issues is very strong, but with scepticism there is always a thread of idealism within it. If you are able to survive on a breath of idealism you should take deep breaths, because I don't want you to give up.

LE

When we tried to map the issues arising from our conversation with Ken, we quickly saw that the discussion was almost totally about global issues.

RB

He took the whole discussion off in a political, rather than ethical or sustainable, direction – talking about the power of designers and the way in which we achieve social change. We did not actually get around to talking about individual design issues at all.

LE

This is perhaps no surprise considering his depth of experience and interests, but his framing of everything as political was interesting. There are many different ways to have these conversations, which is part of the complexity. There is often no consistent use of terms, because the issues are so subjective.

RB

In terms of our mapping process, Ken's conversation resulted in our producing a global and a business context map instead of a design context map, which was actually a good way to start.

LE

Ken talked about business clients, saying that they should not necessarily be trusted because for them money always comes first. But making money isn't necessarily an unethical thing. It's about priorities.

RB

Ken's view of business is revealed by the issues plotted in the business context map, which is imbalanced towards the financial agenda. A sustainable business has to be financially viable, but should be socially and environmentally responsible too.

LE

I liked Ken's suggestion that designers have a 'change of heart', but I'm not clear from our conversation exactly how individual designers might go about that. Our lack of a design context map does not help…

RB

Instead of the 'hearts' approach, there's a logical 'heads' argument to being more sustainable. Whether you behave more sustainably because you want to or because you have to, the starting point is surely an awareness of the relevant issues.

LE

Certainly, if more designers were as well informed about global issues and as personally connected to them as Ken, they would perhaps choose to behave more sustainably.

for thoughts on…

→ **102**
Moral language

→ **117**
**Michael Marriott
on capitalism**

→ **127**
**Simon Esterson
on 'clean' clients**

Given the political focus
of Bassett and Elvins'
discussions with Garland
the resulting maps are
a global context map, left,
and a business context map,
right. The design context
map, bottom, remains blank.

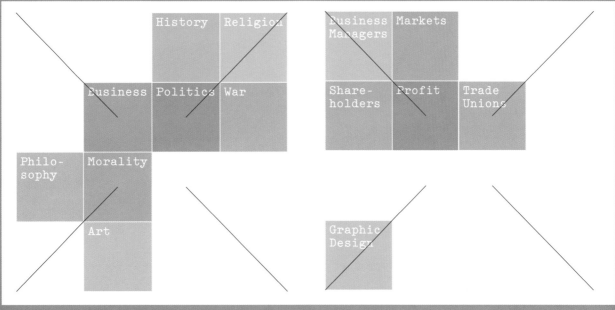

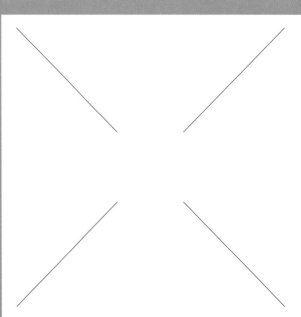

**Metal pipe shop
Calcutta, India**
1998
Garland's photograph
documents a man and his
stock within an economy
where nothing, however rusty,
is ever wasted. Is he a pathetic
relic of the past or a good
example for all our recycled
futures?

Hulger
2004–present
Hulger phones, based on vintage handsets, plug into a mobile or work via bluetooth technology. The logo reflects the curly wire on the handsets. One colour is used per handset box, for cost and to distinguish Hulger from its competitors. The graphic, abstract approach used on the packaging merges the phones' distinctive and beautiful profiles with the logo.

Graphic Japan
2004
The design of this book reflects a country that fuses nostalgia with constant reinvention. The text signatures use three types of uncoated paper and a single colour, magenta. In contrast, the image signatures are glossy and full colour. The cover took this juxtaposition further.

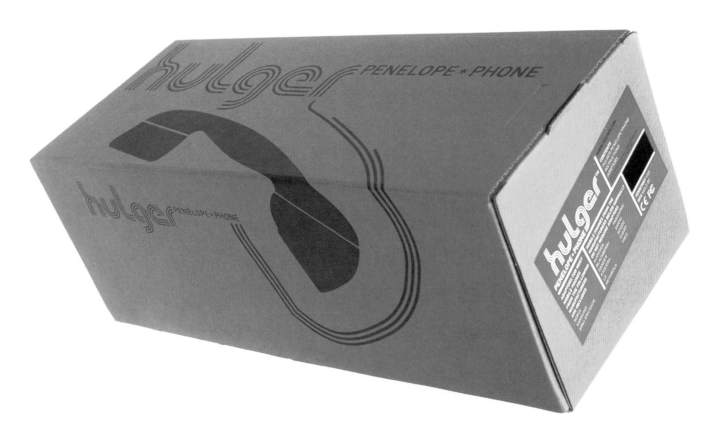

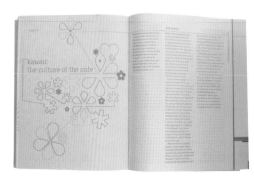

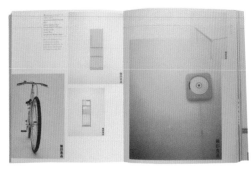

for thoughts on...

→ **088–093**
Deciding who to work for

→ **118**
Michael Marriott
on design insecurity

→ **140**
Sheila Levrant de Bretteville
on moral superiority

VB

I can't help feeling that mapping sustainability issues may work better for a field such as product design, rather than graphic design. I went through and looked at the words being offered, and for some my reaction was irritation… Words like 'well-being' for example, I don't find very helpful because it's so vague. I thought about redefining the terms, but then I realised that adding my own level of interpretation wasn't a productive route to take, as it's the rigidity of the map that should highlight the differences between us all.

You could map four of my projects and they would each be very different. Trying to think of issues that I consider as a designer becomes difficult, because it is so dependent on what each brief requires. I found that the best approach to providing a snapshot of my working process was to work in a reverse manner, deleting words based on frequency. If I rarely considered them, they were out.

Being faced with all these issues in one go also made me feel apprehensive. Going through them made me realise that I don't think about many of them in relation to my work. Looking at issues like biodegradability made me think 'I don't do that, should I be?'. But then when I'm told that biodegradability isn't being considered by most designers, I think, 'Okay, I don't have to feel too bad about not doing that one'.

Being questioned about what I do and how I do it makes me feel quite exposed. One concern I have is about what this will project about myself to others. For example, my magazine work is about communication and content, but heavily led by the visual layout – and potentially this might be regarded as being superficial. The reality is that I have to make decisions without considering all the wider issues. But on a personal level, I like to think that I do think about many of these things. In that way, this discussion makes me question what I do, and why I do it. That's quite scary, but potentially positive.

If I were a student I think I would feel very differently about this conversation – students have yet to commit or define, and can change. I have made a decision to work as a commercial artist. In that sense, I take my lead from a third party, a brief, and I work within the parameters of that brief. It feels as if I need two maps. One would be what I do and the other would be what I could do if money/time was no object. They would of course be very different, because lots of areas in design are out of my control.

It is a sweeping comment, but I would say that sustainability or ethics do not feature in the sphere I personally work in. Although there are values that I have, I respond to a brief. If a client wants a magazine I might suggest a book, a newspaper or push them in a slightly different direction to meet their visual/economic needs, but I wouldn't suggest a completely different object. For me, the biggest decision exists in accepting or declining the brief.

Potentially lots of designers would consider more issues, but they are not given the opportunity from the outset.

RB

It was interesting that our conversation with Violetta stayed entirely within the design context. She was very focused on the individual design issues, quickly identifying one set that were familiar, while recognising another set that were either unfamiliar or irrelevant to her.

LE

She saw the domination of the business context as a necessary reality and conceded that it simply dictates the design brief. However, she wasn't negative about that relationship. She was not surprised that the map revealed an imbalance towards the financial agenda.

RB

Unlike Ken and Pat, Violetta didn't talk about issues on a global scale. Unlike Dan, she separated herself as a person from herself as a working designer.

LE

I liked Violetta's point about how this would all have been easier if she were a student. Retro-fitting sustainability to designers is perhaps too difficult, and will only lead down a path of guilt or criticism. Students are freer to explore and take on new ideas.

RB

We have certainly had more success with students. How do we talk to designers about sustainability without making them feel guilty?

LE

And are designers even in a position to make a difference? Can they go out and change the world? Perhaps the problem is not making designers feel guilty, but making designers feel powerless, which is just as unpleasant.

RB

If the client writes the design brief, designers don't have the opportunity to exercise any influence in these matters. Designers must do more to ensure that clients put sustainability issues on the brief.

LE

But this suggests that designers are currently too reactive. A central part of being a good designer is not merely doing as you are told. You must think about the questions as well as the solutions.

RB

They must become more proactive about sustainability issues. I really don't support the line of defence that 'I'd do more if only I was asked'. The question is, how many designers would know how to do more if they were asked?

for thoughts on...

→ **049**
Jacqueline Roach
on professionalism

→ **094–099**
Work and happiness

→ **118**
Michael Marriott
on design education

icon
2003–present
In this architecture and design magazine, Boxill takes a playful but considered approach to typography. The opening copy is used as headline and standfirst, flexible column widths balance the imagery.

As her map shows, Boxill focused entirely on the design context, quickly identifying the design issues that were important and familiar to her in her practice.

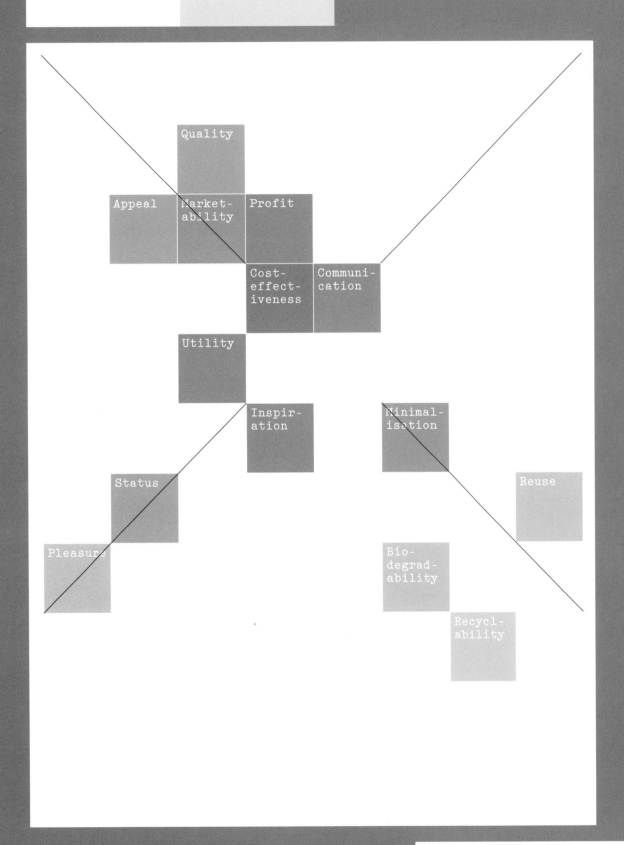

2

How to avoid an appeal – by making a good application

**Cover and spreads,
Representation at
Immigration Appeals:
a best practice guide**
2005
Kahn focuses on making
complex information
as clear and accessible as
possible. This guide was
produced by the Immigration
Law Practitioners' Association
in association with the
Office of the Immigration
Services Commissioner.

Appealing against a negative immigration decision is stressful, can be slow, and will be expensive either for the appellant or for the legal aid budget. It is far better to avoid the appeal process entirely by ensuring the initial application is made properly and the application, whether to the Home Office or to an entry clearance officer, is likely to result in a sustainable decision. Time spent by an adviser before an application is made, ensuring that the applicant, or the relative in the UK, understands what is required and has prepared all the relevant evidence, including original documents (translated as required), will save time later.

How to make an application

Applications may be made

- for entry clearance – to British embassies and high commissions abroad
- for leave to enter – at a British airport or sea port
- for leave to remain in the UK – to the Home Office.

Find out the circumstances

Establish what the real issue is. It may not be presented to you as an immigration problem although it may be; and what result is actually wanted either in the short or long term.

■ EXAMPLE

A person may ask for help because she has been refused child tax credits and wants to appeal to the Department for Work and Pensions – but the problem may really be that she does not have an immigration status which allows her to obtain these benefits.

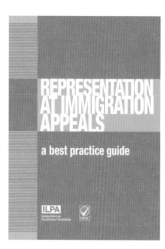

for thoughts on...

→ 056
**Richard Holloway
on making a difference**

→ 088–093
Designer responsibility

→ 138
**Sheila Levrant de Bretteville
on self-interest**

PK

As a designer, I'm midway between publishing organisations and their readers. I work within a chain of processes which links originator to editor, through me to printer and distributor. My main tasks are to turn text into reader-friendly documents and to smooth production for the rest of the chain.

The clients I work for are nearly all in the voluntary or campaigning sectors. Some are human rights organisations with ethical concerns the subject of their publications. Some things I work on, such as handbooks on immigration law, seem as if they might make a difference to someone's life – in getting asylum-seekers out of detention, say. This is relatively rare in print work and makes the work a pleasure.

My clients don't have design departments or much production expertise. They are usually overstretched and have little idea about what happens between their final Word document and the finished publication. My role is to explain, to troubleshoot, to smooth relations and procedures. I work to produce the best design possible within time and budget. For me that means a publication that is readable, appealing, clear and error-free.

I help these groups represent themselves authoritatively to their readers and in a style in keeping with their aims. I'm often the first general reader of text that can contain garbled-in-committee prose, stylistic inconsistencies or unspotted glitches. The important thing is improving the clarity of what is to be read and helping to carry through the author's intentions. Mostly I help my clients to organise things. I think about ways that readers can find their way around a document.

Gimmicky design drives me crazy, especially if information is the main point. Why should a website have Flash pages with no function? If you want 'bells and whistles' that's fine, but I believe you have to knit design with the basics of organising information to ensure a publication gets to the widest audience. I would say that is an ethical responsibility.

In order to be readable, documents also have to be interesting. But what I guess people think of as conventional design choices – what typeface? what paper? – come in to my work pretty minimally. If there were more money available, my clients would probably consider these elements more. They take pleasure in something looking well produced, but are nervous about spending money on what might be viewed as unnecessary. In that way, they don't understand how design works – what those things can do and what else design is about.

So much of the design and production process is invisible, especially now that it happens on computers rather than not so long ago when cutting and pasting literally meant pasting things down. Print production for me is now about social organisation of the people involved.

Sometimes I make documents more durable by laminating, but I don't know how that affects the environmental aspects. In terms of the environmental agenda, a good starting point is whether something is necessary in the first place. I think it's important to think of these issues in that broad sense. At a repro house, I worked on the kind of inserts that fall out of weekend newspapers. They had amazingly complicated visuals and technical specs to get just right: perforations and scratch-off panels and glued areas. But I knew, and everybody else knew, that you get these things and mostly throw them straight in the bin. That is the opposite of environmental and I would like to see more discussion at that level.

RB

The conversation with Pat involved global and business issues, as well as discussing the design context.

LE

Interestingly, the majority of our conversation with Pat was about the relationship between designer and client.

RB

The maps that we produced after meeting Pat reveal the emphasis of the management of her work with 'social clients'. Financial issues do not feature so much, because the commercial success of the work is not so central to her interpretation of the brief.

LE

The mapping also reflects Pat's opinion that personal issues are not as relevant in her work. Also, while she is very much aware of environmental issues, she didn't feel that there is much opportunity within design briefs to act upon them.

RB

Pat suggested that creating more sustainable design was more dependent on clients than designers.

LE

At the moment, if you do want to be more sustainable you have got to ensure that you find an appropriate client.

RB

This might mean becoming your own client or finding clients that already have clear social or environmental objectives.

LE

The challenge arises if you wish to behave more sustainably for a client that has not already asked for it. We are asking designers to become advocates, negotiators or persuaders. Maybe we are asking them to become something they are not?

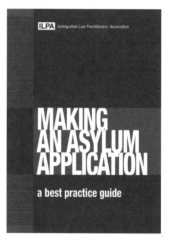

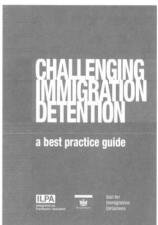

for thoughts on...

→ **055**
Richard Holloway
on humility

→ **086**
Inclusivity

→ **116**
Michael Marriott
on the differences between
artists and designers

Kahn's discussions with
Bassett and Elvins resulted
in all three context maps:
global context, left;
business context, right;
design context, shown
bottom right.

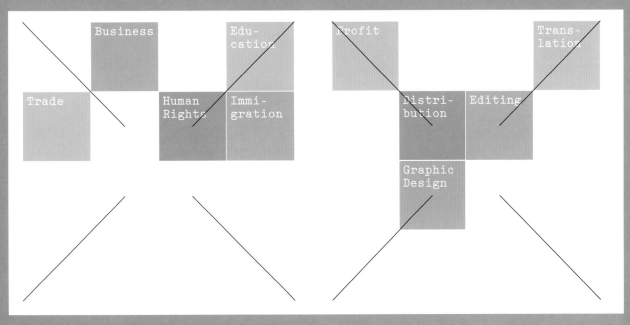

**Covers, Making an
Asylum Application
and Challenging
Immigration Detention**
2002, 2003
Kahn used strong colour to
differentiate between the
covers in this series of best
practice guides designed
for the Immigration Law
Practitioners' Association
and Bail for Immigration
Detainees.

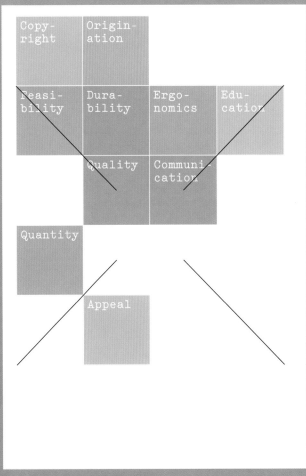

10.2 Multi-Ply Coffee Table
2000
Eatock collaborated with the architect Sam Solhaug to design this table. One of their self-imposed parameters was that the table should use an entire 8 x 4 feet sheet of plywood. Eatock acknowledges that this was more a practical and conceptual challenge than an environmental one.

Eye logo and graphic identity, Big Brother 7
2006
The Big Brother logo conceals a secret message – an exciting, interactive yet stealthy method of distribution. This is revealed if viewers stare at the centre of the spiral, slightly defocus their eyes, rotate the image clockwise for twenty seconds and then stare at a light coloured area.

for thoughts on...

DE

I don't consider myself a conventional graphic designer. I make work for myself and others, making some projects for profit, and others for no profit at all. So, for me to position an issue like profit becomes almost impossible.

My own work often starts with a question or simple observation. The starting point for designing the 10.2 Multi-Ply Coffee Table was to use an entire 8 x 4 sheet of plywood. I collaborated with an architect and we established a set of parameters, one being that there be no material wasted. Creating a cutting pattern without waste was a challenge based on efficiency and maximisation of the material. The system generated the form. We did not have an environmental agenda, yet a lot of people had interest in the table from that viewpoint. A lot of labour is needed to make the table, so although there is no waste in materials there is a lot of time required to build one. It was not designed to be manufactured, it was an investigation in pattern making and materials. There are other designers and artists working like this, producing things – things that subvert the expected, the material, the context and make you think or smile.

When I work like this there is no brief. I'll see something and think there could be an answer. It's like a collision of things. I'll make observations, and then based on them I'll create a work. The clients I have understand that I work in this way and ask me to apply my thinking to their needs.

If I start thinking about commissioned work, profit is always right in the middle, so is communication. Cost-effectiveness, from the client's perspective, that's what they want. Innovation is often talked about in terms of doing something new, if it's possible within the budget. Clients tend to present a problem, such as 'we have a new programme', and need to tell people using billboards. I can then think about what might be possible within those parameters. But there is so much that just goes unsaid. I often don't get written briefs. They just say 'what would you do with this?'.

When I produce printed materials I do think about recycling. To me it's obvious that you choose recycled, or at least research the stock. But I also design advertisements for magazines and then I have no control over the paper. If I were only creating 500 postcards, I would ask the printer if they have some left over stock or spare space on the margins of another job. In that sense I am recycling, but it's not going on recycled stock. I just do this, but I don't think of it as considering recycling as an isolated issue.

As a designer/artist everything I do just constantly involves issues, whether it's what I design or what I do this weekend. It's about the way I live. But looking at all these issues, it's the social ones I haven't thought about much. Disability, security or emerging economies, those are all issues I haven't dealt with yet, but I think I understand what they mean.

RB

It would have been almost impossible to create a single map to describe Dan's activity as it is so wide-ranging. Instead these two overlapping maps give some clear insight into how Dan balances his design projects.

LE

The Big Brother project is far more commercial and, unsurprisingly, has an imbalance towards the financial agenda. The postcard project, being self-initiated, is more weighted towards the personal agenda.

RB

Dan was very keen to have 'fun' in his work, and this issue also features on each map. But how do we remind designers to think about 'disability' and 'poverty' at the same time?

LE

In spite of the differences in the two briefs, Dan has positioned the issues of 'awareness' and 'innovation' centrally on both project maps.

RB

It would be good to see this happen on more design projects: the challenge for designers is to become aware of more issues, without this becoming a barrier to innovation.

LE

The best innovators often work better when they are faced with restrictions. When a client produces an open design brief, the designers often impose their own constraints in order to make progress.

RB

That said, a more open approach would create opportunities to address more issues and hopefully result in more sustainable design.

Postcard Back Compositions

1. Archetypal
2. Reflected
3. Opposite
4. Portrait
5. Big Message Small Address
6. Small Message Big Address
7. Disjointed

Daniel Eatock   1 /1000
First Edition Published 2006
ISBN 0-9551104-1-3

for thoughts on...

→ 106–111
The value of design

→ 116
**Michael Marriott
on the differences between
artists and designers**

→ 123
**Billie Tsien
on transience**

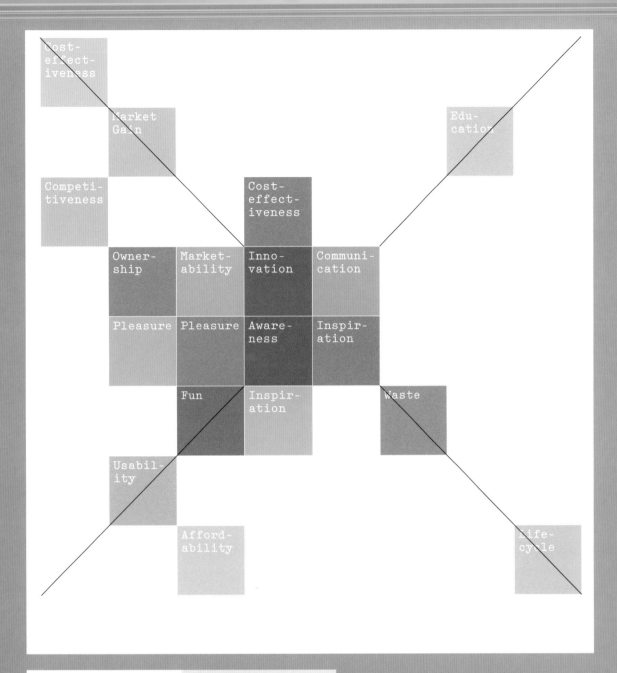

**Envelope and postcard
back compositions**
2006
This set of seven postcards
was inspired by George
Maciunas who used the skills
and methods of a commercial
graphic designer to make
and promote non elitist art for
all. The detritus of the Fluxus
movement is an inspiration
and reminder that we as
graphic designers can initiate,
contribute and introduce our
own ideas into the world
without waiting for a client's
commission.

Eatock's work encompasses
the highly commercial
and art-based projects. By
overlaying two design context
maps Bassett and Elvins have
explored the relationship
between these two areas of
his practice.

This last section explores how Rupert Bassett and Lynne Elvins' Sustainability Issue Mapping helps designers to understand the ethical dimensions of their work and develop practical ways forward. By charting design work against this mapping tool, it is easy to see that most of us are rather imbalanced in our ethical approach to design.

The first step towards trying to be ethical is being socially aware and engaged. Although ours is a small contribution in a big world, this isn't an excuse for apathy or for abdicating responsibility. It is a peculiarity of design that practitioners feel simultaneously powerful and disempowered. The design community feels itself to be important, but designers often consider their hands tied by client constraint. Perhaps this conflict needs to be addressed more forcibly. Design is a service, but what this service encompasses is open to review.

Graphic design is a powerful tool because it is crucial in the communication of messages. It has a role in persuading, educating and delighting others. As Dan Eatock said, design can make you think and smile – as we have seen throughout this book, both are ethical concerns. Although not unaware of the possible aesthetic pleasures derived from design work, Pat Kahn is focused on using her skill to make the world a more accessible place – the ideal being to achieve both.

Designers are usually in a responsive position, reacting to problems set by clients within timeframes and budgets not of the designer's making. For Violetta Boxill this means that the most significant decision a designer makes is whether to take on a job or not.

Finding mutually respectful and receptive clients, whose messages we are happy to help convey, is all-important. So is encouraging an open debate between client and designer about ethics in design work. To do this, designers need to demonstrate that they are aware of business constraints while framing discussions within a larger ethical context. As designers we play a part in the present economic system that looks set to have devastating environmental consequences. Designers are trained to think laterally in order to solve problems. We are now all being called upon to solve a very big problem. There are different forms of engagement open to us. As Ken Garland advocates, one is political. We should all vote, for example – even a spoiled ballot paper is counted as a comment after all. Perhaps value needs to be placed differently so that we are proud to be well-informed citizens of the world, just as much as members of the design community.

'The personal is the political' was the mantra of the 1970s and is just as relevant today. As Dan Eatock said, design decisions reflect your ethos – the way you choose to live. Recognising that there is a relationship between personal and professional ethics is empowering – change is not necessarily a top-down thing. Violetta Boxill was particularly honest in saying that change can nevertheless be hard, particularly for designers who are already embedded in the system. She thinks that students are in the best position to challenge the status quo. So, could it be over to you?

Suggested reading

Each principal interviewee was asked to compile a short reading list of five books. Specific editions of widely published titles have been included only when recommended by the people featured in this list.

Chris de Bode

Ryszard Kapuscinski
Imperium

Heinrich Harrer
die Weisse Spinne (the White Spider)

Richard Avedon
An Autobiography
Random House Inc, USA
1993

Don McCullin
Sleeping with Ghosts

James Nachtwey
Deeds of War
Thames & Hudson
1989

Sheila Levrant de Bretteville

Marshall Berman
All That is Solid Melts into Air:
The Experience of Modernity
Penguin Books Ltd, New York
1982

Hal Foster
The Return of the Real:
Art and Theory at the End of the Century
The MIT Press
1996

Elliot Perlman
Seven Types of Ambiguity
Penguin Books Ltd, New York
2003

Naomi Schor
Reading in Detail, Aesthetics and
the Feminine
Methuen, New York
1987

Cornel West
Race Matters
Random House
1993

Simon Esterson

Robin Kinross
Modern Typography:
An Essay in Critical History
Hyphen Press
2nd edition 2004

Richard Hollis
Swiss Graphic Design:
The Origins and Growth of an
International Style,
1920–1965
Laurence King Publishing
2006

William Owen
Magazine Design
Laurence King Publishing
1991

Steven Bach
Final Cut:
Art, Money and Ego in the
Making of 'Heaven's Gate',
the Film That Sank United Artists
Newmarket Press, USA
1999

Felicity Lawrence
Not on the Label:
What Really Goes into the Food on Your Plate
Penguin Books Ltd
2004

Anthony Grayling

Simon Blackburn
Being Good:
A Short Introduction to Ethics
Oxford Paperbacks
2003

Aristotle
The Nichomachean Ethics
(any standard English translation,
eg as published by Penguin Books Ltd)

José Luis Bermúdez and Sebastian Gardner
(editors)
Art and Morality
Routledge
2002

Jerrold Levinson (editor)
Aesthetics and Ethics:
Essays at the Intersection
(Cambridge Studies in
Philosophy & the Arts)
Cambridge University Press
1998

Stephen Davies (editor)
Art and its Messages:
Meaning, Morality and Society
Pennsylvania State University Press
1997

Richard Holloway

Isaiah Berlin
The Proper Study of Mankind:
An Anthology of Essays
Chatto and Windus
1997

Richard Holloway
Godless Morality:
Keeping Religion out of Ethics
Canongate Press
2000

Richard Holloway
Looking in the Distance
Canongate Press
2004

Friedrich Nietzsche, RJ Hollingdale (translator)
Beyond Good and Evil
Penguin Books Ltd
1990

Friedrich Nietzsche
On the Genealogy of Morals

Michael Marriott

Charles Jencks and Nathan Silver
Adhocism:
The Case for Improvisation
Doubleday Publishing, New York
1972

Norman Potter
What is a Designer:
Things, Places, Messages
Hyphen Press
2002

Robert M Pirsig
Zen and The Art of Motorcycle Maintenance:
(An Inquiry into Values)

Peter Zumthor
Thinking Architecture
Birkhäuser Verlag AG
1999

Delyth Morgan

Anthony Giddens, Patrick Diamond
The New Egalitarianism
Polity Press
2005

Richard Layard
Happiness:
Lessons From a New Science
Penguin Books Ltd
2006

Anthony Trollope
The Warden
Oxford University Press
1998

Margaret Atwood
The Handmaid's Tale
Vintage
1996

Graham Greene
Monsignor Quixote
Vintage
2005

Jacqueline Roach

Harper Lee
To Kill a Mockingbird

John Mortimer
Any Rumpole novel

Charlotte Bronte
Jane Eyre

Toni Morrison
Beloved

AS Byatt
Possession: A Romance

Billie Tsien

Vladimir Nabokov
Speak, Memory

MFK Fisher
The Art of Eating
Wiley Publishing Inc
1937

Wendell Barry
What Are People For? (essays)
HarperCollins Canada
1990

Virginia Woolf
To the Lighthouse

Mary Oliver
When Death Comes (poem)
in Mary Oliver, New and Selected Poems
Beacon Press USA
1992

Julian Baggini
Making Sense:
Philosophy behind the Headlines
Oxford University Press
2002

Simon Blackburn
Being Good:
A Short Introduction to Ethics
Oxford Paperbacks
2003

Alain de Botton
On Seeing and Noticing
Penguin Books Ltd
2005

Alain de Botton
Status Anxiety
Penguin Books Ltd
2004

Anthony Grayling
The Meaning of Things
Phoenix Press
2002

Anthony Grayling
What is Good?
Phoenix Press
2004

Steven Heller and Véronique Vienne (editors)
Citizen Designer:
Perspectives on Design Responsibility
Allworth Press
2003

Richard Holloway
Godless Morality:
Keeping Religion out of Ethics
Canongate Press
2000

Richard Koch and Chris Smith
Suicide of the West
Continuum
2006

Richard Layard
Happiness:
Lessons From a New Science
Penguin Books Ltd
2006

Lucienne Roberts trained as a graphic designer at the Central School of Art and Design, London, UK. Having been inspired by the political engagement of the early modernists, Roberts was motivated to work in areas loosely defined as political and social. After a brief period at publishers The Women's Press, she established the design studio sans+baum, where clients have ranged from arts organisations to NGOs and charities. Roberts has taught at Middlesex University and the London College of Communication. She was a signatory of the First Things First 2000 manifesto and a judge for the ISTD awards 2001. sans+baum projects were included in the exhibition Communicate: Independent British Graphic Design since the Sixties held at the Barbican, London. Her recent books include **Drip-dry Shirts: The evolution of the graphic designer (2005).** [British, born 1962]

Rebecca Wright studied sculpture and then graphic design at Bath College of Higher Education before attending the Royal College of Art, London, UK, where she gained her masters degree in illustration. Wright's practice reflects her interest in reading, writing and design. She runs a letterpress workshop where she produces printed matter and small edition publications for a range of private and commercial clients, and she writes and lectures on visual communication and design. She is currently working on a project investigating the role of vernacular design in passing on traditions, history and stories within families and community groups. Wright has taught at colleges throughout the UK and is senior lecturer in graphic media design at the London College of Communication. [British, born 1972]

Ray Roberts graduated from the Central School of Arts and Crafts, London, UK in 1947. After working under Oliver Simon at the Curwen Press, he set up his own design practice in 1961. Believing in graphic design as a valuable tool for mass communication, Roberts's clients were diverse. He designed publicity for the British Transport Commission, posters for the Arts Council, catalogues for the Wallace Collection in London, books for Tate Gallery Publications and information manuals for National Westminster Bank. He has taught at a number of British colleges and universities including the Central School of Art and Design, Middlesex University and the University of Reading. In keeping with many of his generation, Roberts remains as broadly engaged with his subject today as he was during the 50 years of his working life. [British, born 1925]

The biographical details of all interviewees are included near to their contribution.

Rupert Bassett studied at Ravensbourne College of Design and Communication and the Royal College of Art before setting up his own design studio specialising in corporate information design. Committed to the aesthetics and principles of modernism, Bassett's approach to design is structured and rational. He has worked on visual identities for GlaxoWellcome, the RAC, and the BT Talk Zone exhibition at the Millennium Dome. Bassett is the designer for SustainAbility, an independent international think tank advising on corporate responsibility and sustainable development, where he met Lynne Elvins. [British, born 1965]

Lynne Elvins studied design management at Surrey Institute of Art and Design before working for SustainAbility where she researched how companies and activists communicate sustainability issues using the internet. An independent consultant, Elvins has worked with the Design Council, csrnetwork and the Centre for Sustainable Design for whom she co-authored a report on the marketing of green goods for the Japanese Ministry of Trade and Economy. She has lectured on sustainable design and design management, is editor of Radar, SustainAbility's bi-monthly publication and is a Fellow of the Royal Society of Arts. [British, born 1971]

Elvins and Bassett formed **A420,** an exploratory design and research unit, to provide the design industry with a simple visual way to navigate the complex subject of sustainability. They devised Sustainability Issue Mapping (SIM) as a systematic method to reveal the opportunities, risks and issues involved in sustainable design.

production
John McGill

index
Indexing Specialists (UK) Ltd

**inside front/back covers,
009, 018/019, 035, 045, 051,
059, 164, 166, 168, 174, 175**
photography Dave Shaw

022

**King Akhenaten and
Queen Nefertiti**
BPK/Ägyptisches Museum
und Papyrussammlung,
Staatliche Museen Berlin
photography Margarete Büsing

Statue of Buddha
© Spectrum/Heritage-Images

Illustration of tiles
copy photography by
Ian Bavington Jones

Misericord
by permission of the
Dean and Canons of Windsor

**Pieter de Hooch
A Woman Peeling Apples**
reproduced by kind
permission of the trustees of
The Wallace Collection, London

023

**Joseph Wright of Derby
The Orrery**
Derby Museum and Art Gallery,
UK/The Bridgeman Art Library

027

**Engraving,
The Abolitionist League**
private collection, London

Cartoon, James Gillray
private collection, London

**Programme cover,
National American Women's
Suffrage Association**
Library of Congress,
Washington [Prints and
Photographs Collection/
Women's Suffrage]
LC-USZC4-2996

Cover, The Masses
courtesy of the Michigan
State University Libraries/
American Radicalism Collection

030

**Poster, USSR
Agricultural Exhibition**
© DACS 2006

Weissenhof settlement
AKG-Images/Electa

Poster, Abram Games
estate of Abram Games

Cover, First Things First
reproduced courtesy of
Ken Garland

Photograph, Nick Ut
© EMPICS/AP

031

AIDS symbol
reproduced courtesy of
Milton Glaser

Shelter logo
reproduced courtesy of
Shelter

Greenpeace logo
reproduced courtesy of
Greenpeace

Why Iraq? Why Now?
reproduced courtesy of
Alan Kitching

082–111

Demos policy statement
relating to use of extracts from
Demos publications:

'Demos publications are
available free for download.
We allow anyone to access our
content electronically without
charge. We want to encourage
the circulation of our work as
widely as possible without
affecting the ownership of the
copyright, which remains with
the copyright holder.'

www.demos.co.uk

082–111

Copyright of extracts remains
with the original author.

100/101, 106/107
illustration Nigel Robinson

122/123, 148/149

Neurosciences
Research Institute/American
Folk Art Museum
photography Michael Moran

132/133, 154/155

© Chris de Bode/Panos Pictures

136/137, 156/157, 158/159

**Remembering old
Little Tokyo**
photography Annette del Zoppo

**At the Start...
At Long Last...**
photography Lewis Tanner

**Out to lunch...
Back to work...**
photography Henk vanAssen

161–191

Sustainability Issue Mapping
© 2006
Lynne Elvins and
Rupert Bassett of A420
All rights reserved

163

photography Rupert Bassett
and Lynne Elvins

176, 178

photography Ken Garland

180

photography Nicolas Roope

188

Big Brother
photography David Grandorge

...book like this is impossible
to produce without the support
of others. Thank you to all
the interviewees who gave
their time so generously
and patiently.

Thank you to Brian Morris and
Natalia Price-Cabrera at AVA
for giving me this opportunity
and for being hugely supportive
throughout.

Particular thanks are due to
Dave Shaw, Rebecca Wright,
John McGill, Lorna Fray and
Malcolm Southward all of
whom have been great friends
as well as helpers. Thank you
also to Bob Wilkinson,
Deirdre Murphy and Ruth Scott.

I want to thank above all
Putzi and Ray Roberts, my
parents, and Damian Wayling,
whose friendship cannot be
bettered.